Laboratory Manual
to accompany

Eighth Edition

puntos
de partida

An Invitation to Spanish

María Sabló-Yates
Delta College

McGraw-Hill
Higher Education

Boston   Burr Ridge, IL   Dubuque, IA   New York
San Francisco   St. Louis   Bangkok   Bogotá   Caracas   Kuala Lumpur
Lisbon   London   Madrid   Mexico City   Milan   Montreal   New Delhi
Santiago   Seoul   Singapore   Sydney   Taipei   Toronto

McGraw-Hill
Higher Education

Laboratory Manual to accompany
Puntos de partida: An Invitation to Spanish, Eighth Edition

3 4 5 6 7 8 9 WDQ/WDQ 0

ISBN: 978-0-07-332550-7
MHID: 0-07-332550-3

Vice President and Editor-in-Chief: *Michael J. Ryan*
Publisher: *William R. Glass*
Executive Editor: *Christa Harris*
Director of Development: *Scott Tinetti*
Development Editors: *Mara Brown and Allen J. Bernier*
Marketing Manager: *Jorge Arbujas*
Production Editor: *Alison Meier*
Editorial Assistant: *Margaret Young*
Production Supervisor: *Louis Swaim*
Composition: *Palatino by Aptara, Inc.*
Printing: *40# Alt Book 690 by Worldcolor*
Illustrators: *Wayne Clark, David Bohn, Axelle Fortier, Lori Heckelman, Judith Macdonald, Stephanie O'Shaughnessy, Barbara Reinerison, Katherine Tillotson, Stan Tusan, and Joe Veno.*

The Internet addresses listed in the text were accurate at the time of publication. The inclusion of a Web site does not indicate an endorsement by the authors or McGraw-Hill, and McGraw-Hill does not guarantee the accuracy of the information presented at these sites.

Realia Credits: *Page 186* © Joaquín Salvador Lavado (QUINO) *Toda Mafalda*—Ediciones de La Flor, 1993; *209* Cartoon by Bob Schroeter

Contents

To the Student

The purpose of the audio program that accompanies *Puntos de partida* is to give you as much practice as possible in listening to, speaking, reading, and writing, and, above all, understanding the Spanish language in a variety of contexts. This edition of the Laboratory Manual contains a variety of exercises to help you accomplish that goal. To get the most out of the audio program, you should listen to the CDs or the online audio program after your instructor covers the corresponding material in class, and you should listen as often as possible. You will need the Laboratory Manual much of the time when you listen to the audio program since many of the exercises are based on visuals, realia (real things—such as advertisements, classified ads, and so on—that you would encounter in a Spanish-speaking country), and written cues.

The audio program follows the format of chapters in the main text. Each chapter begins with a section (**Vocabulario: Preparación**) in which you can practice vocabulary in a variety of contexts. This preliminary vocabulary study is followed by pronunciation exercises (**Pronunciación y ortografía**). Each chapter includes exercises to practice the grammatical concepts of the chapters (**Gramática**) and functional dialogue (**Videoteca: Minidramas**). In addition, there is a section that combines grammar points and vocabulary introduced in the chapter (**Un poco de todo: Para entregar**). This section is to be handed in to your instructor for correction; no answers are provided on the audio program, or in the answers Appendix at the back of the Laboratory Manual. In addition, some exercises give you the option of answering in writing. Since writing the answers to these exercises is an option only, you should ask your instructor how she or he would prefer these to be handled. Finally, each chapter concludes with a brief quiz (**Prueba corta**). Each quiz allows you to check your mastery of the vocabulary and grammatical structures learned in that specific chapter.

The exercises in most sections progress from controlled to more open-ended and personalized or interactive, to give you a chance to be more creative in Spanish while practicing the skills you have learned. With the exception of the **Para entregar** portions of the Laboratory Manual, the **Dictados,** and other writing-based exercises, you will hear the answers to most exercises immediately after the item or at the end of a series of items. You will find the answers to most written exercises (except those called **Para entregar**) in the Appendix.

Although the audio program includes some material taken directly from *Puntos de partida,* it also contains many new exercises: surveys (**Encuestas**); dictations; personalized questions and interviews; visually based listening comprehension exercises; cultural listening passages, some based on survey questions answered by native speakers; exercises based on realia; and brief interactive dialogues. Whenever possible, the exercises are presented in a context.

The following types of exercises are a regular feature of the *Puntos de partida* audio program and are found in most chapters.

- **Definiciones, Situaciones,** and **Asociaciones** use a multiple choice or matching format in order to test listening comprehension and vocabulary.
- **Identificaciones** and **Descripción,** as their names imply, will ask you to generate responses based on visuals, with or without written or oral cues. Although these are more controlled in nature, they are contextualized and related to the theme of the current or a previous chapter. You will find these types of exercises throughout the Laboratory Manual.
- **Encuestas** are personalized surveys in which you need only check an answer that is true for you. These surveys are offered for listening comprehension and are related to the theme of the chapter or to specific grammar points. You will find these at the beginning of both the vocabulary and the grammar sections.
- **Los hispanos hablan** is found after **Vocabulario: Preparación** and presents comments from native speakers on a variety of topics: clothing, pastimes, favorite foods, and so on. Each section of **Los hispanos hablan** is tied to the theme and/or the vocabulary of the chapter in which it is found. The passages offer listening comprehension that is based on cultural information. The follow-up activities include taking notes, evaluating true or false statements, making comparisons, completing charts, and answering questions.

- The **Gramática en acción** presentations appear at the beginning of each grammar section. These brief conversations and paragraphs offer real-life examples of the corresponding grammar points. The **Gramática en acción** sections are identical to those found in *Puntos de partida*. The follow-up exercises include cloze dictations, true or false statements, identifying the person who made a statement, inferring information from the dialogue, and writing information about the dialogue (in **¿Qué recuerdas?**).
- There are two types of question and answer sequences. The first will offer you an oral or written cue, and you will hear the correct answer after each item. **Entrevista** activities, in contrast, offer no cues or answers. The questions are more open-ended and personalized, and you will be able to pause the CD or the audio program to write your answers. The **Entrevista** is a regular feature of the **Un poco de todo** section that is for handing in to your instructor.
- The **Videoteca: Minidramas** dialogues are taken from the DVD to accompany *Puntos de partida*, which is available to adopters and their students. Like the **Gramática en acción** presentations, they offer examples of real-life conversations and situations, as well as some cultural information. After they are read, you will usually have the opportunity to participate in a similar conversation, interactive in nature, in which you use the cues that are provided. In some instances, you may have the option of writing your answers. You will always hear a correct answer. In earlier chapters, you will have the opportunity to repeat portions of the dialogue.
- Listening passages appear in the **Un poco de todo** section. These passages are cultural in nature and contain information on a variety of topics related to the Hispanic world. Their themes are related to the theme of each chapter. The passages are usually preceded by a section called **Antes de escuchar** in which you will practice listening strategies: guessing content, gisting, making inferences about the passage, and so on. Following each passage is a **Después de escuchar** section that offers a variety of comprehension or follow-up exercises.
- The Laboratory Manual also includes many types of dictations (**Dictados**) and other writing activities. You will be asked to listen for and write down specific information: letters, words, phrases, or entire sentences. In some instances, you will be asked to jot down notes about the content of brief passages. Answers are generally provided in the Appendix.

Sound effects are used throughout the audio program, when appropriate. You will hear a variety of native speakers, so that you can get used to different accents and voice types found in the Spanish-speaking world, but no accent will be so pronounced as to be difficult for you to understand. In approximately the first third of the audio program, the speakers will speak at a slower rate. The rate of speech will increase gradually until it reaches natural or close to natural speed in the final third of the audio program.

Learning another language requires hard work and patience, as well as an open mind. We hope that the variety of exercises and the cultural information in the Laboratory Manual will provide a natural and stimulating context within which you will begin to communicate in Spanish!

We offer our sincere thanks to the following individuals: to Ana María Pérez-Gironés (Wesleyan University), who wrote the listening passages in **Un poco de todo**; to Manuela González-Bueno, who made many helpful suggestions for improving the **Pronunciación y ortografía** sections; to the Hispanic exchange students whose answers were the bases of the passages in the **Los hispanos hablan**; to William R. Glass, who provided welcome suggestions and advice; to Thalia Dorwick, Christa Harris, Scott Tinetti, Mara Brown, and Allen J. Bernier, whose comments, suggestions, and superior editing made this Laboratory Manual and audio program possible; and to my family for their support and understanding throughout the writing process.

María Sabló-Yates

PRIMERA PARTE

■■■Saludos y expresiones de cortesía

A. Diálogos

Paso 1. In the following dialogues, you will practice greeting others appropriately in Spanish. The dialogues will be read with pauses for repetition. After each dialogue, you will hear two summarizing statements. Circle the letter of the statement that best describes each dialogue. First, listen.

1. MANOLO: ¡Hola, Maricarmen!
    MARICARMEN: ¿Qué tal, Manolo? ¿Cómo estás?
    MANOLO: Muy bien. ¿Y tú?
    MARICARMEN: Regular. Nos vemos, ¿eh?
    MANOLO: Hasta mañana.

    Comprensión: a. b.

2. ELISA VELASCO: Buenas tardes, señor Gómez.
    MARTÍN GÓMEZ: Muy buenas, señora Velasco. ¿Cómo está?
    ELISA VELASCO: Bien, gracias. ¿Y usted?
    MARTÍN GÓMEZ: Muy bien, gracias. Hasta luego.
    ELISA VELASCO: Adiós.

    Comprensión: a. b.

3. LUPE: Buenos días, profesor.
    PROFESOR: Buenos días. ¿Cómo te llamas?
    LUPE: Me llamo Lupe Carrasco.
    PROFESOR: Mucho gusto, Lupe.
    LUPE: Igualmente.

    Comprensión: a. b.

4. MIGUEL: ¡Hola! Me llamo Miguel René. ¿Y tú? ¿Cómo te llamas?
    KARINA: Me llamo Karina. Mucho gusto.
    MIGUEL: Mucho gusto, Karina. Y, ¿de dónde eres?
    KARINA: Yo soy de Venezuela. ¿Y tú?
    MIGUEL: Yo soy de México.

    Comprensión: a. b.

Paso 2. Now you will participate in a conversation, partially printed in your Manual, in which you play the role of Karina. Complete the conversation using the written cues. When you hear the corresponding number, say Karina's line. Then you will hear Miguel's response. Continue until you complete the conversation. (If you wish, pause and write the answers.) Here are the cues for your conversation.

buenas tardes	cómo te llamas	de dónde eres
me llamo	mucho gusto	yo soy

Now, begin the conversation.

KARINA: 1. _____.

MIGUEL: Muy buenas.

KARINA: 2. _____ Karina. 3. ¿_____?

MIGUEL: Me llamo Miguel.

KARINA: 4. _____, Miguel. 5. ¿_____?

MIGUEL: Soy de Puerto Rico. ¿Y tú?

KARINA: 6. _____ de Puerto Rico también.

B. ¿Formal o informal? You will hear a series of expressions. Indicate whether each expression would be used in a formal or in an informal situation.

1. a. formal   b. informal
2. a. formal   b. informal
3. a. formal   b. informal
4. a. formal   b. informal
5. a. formal   b. informal

C. Situaciones

Paso 1. You will hear a series of questions or statements. Each will be said twice. Circle the letter of the best response or reaction to each.

1. a. Me llamo Ricardo Barrios.   b. Bien, gracias.
2. a. Encantada, Eduardo.   b. Muchas gracias, Eduardo.
3. a. Regular. ¿Y tú?   b. Mucho gusto, señorita Paz.
4. a. Con permiso, señor.   b. No hay de qué.
5. a. De nada, señora Colón.   b. Buenas noches, señora Colón.
6. a. Soy de Guatemala.   b. ¿Y tú?

Paso 2. Now, listen to the questions and statements again and read the correct answers in the pauses provided. You will hear each item only once. Be sure to repeat the correct answer after you hear it.

1. ...   2. ...   3. ...   4. ...   5. ...   6. ...

D. ¿Qué dicen estas personas? (*What are these people saying?*) Circle the letter of the drawing that is best described by the sentences you hear. Each will be said twice.

1. a.

    b.

2. a.

    b.

3. a.

    b.

4. a.

    b.

■■■¿Cómo es usted? (Part 1)

A. ¿Cómo es usted? You will hear the following brief conversation. It will be read with pauses for repetition. First, listen to the conversation. (Then repeat as directed.)

—¿Cómo es usted?
—Bueno… Yo soy moderna, independiente, sofisticada…

B. Encuesta (*Survey*). You will hear a series of questions. For each question, check the appropriate answer. No answers will be given. The answers you choose should be correct for you!

1. ☐ Sí, soy independiente.
   ☐ No, no soy independiente.

2. ☐ Sí, soy sentimental.
   ☐ No, no soy sentimental.

3. ☐ Sí, soy eficiente.
   ☐ No, no soy eficiente.

4. ☐ Sí, soy flexible.
   ☐ No, no soy flexible.

C. Descripción. In this exercise, you will practice gisting, that is, getting the main idea—an important skill in language learning. Although some of the vocabulary you hear will not be familiar to you, concentrate on the words that you *do* know. After the exercise, pause and choose the statement that best describes the passage.

1. ☐ This person is describing her country and the sports that are played there.

2. ☐ This person is describing herself, her studies, and her outside interests.

Now resume listening.

D. Preguntas (*Questions*). Ask the following persons about their personalities, using ¿**Eres… ?** or ¿**Es usted… ?** as appropriate, and the cues you will hear. Follow the model. (Remember to repeat the correct question. If you prefer, pause and write the questions.) You will hear answers to your questions.

MODELO: (*you see*) Marcos (*you hear*) tímido →
(*you say*) Marcos ¿eres tímido? (*you hear*) Sí, soy tímido.

1. Ramón, ¿_____?

2. Señora Alba, ¿_____?

3. Señor Castán, ¿_____?

4. Anita, ¿_____?

E. Dictado: ¿Cómo son? (*What are they like?*) You will hear five sentences. Each will be said twice. Listen carefully and write the missing words. (Check your answers in the Appendix.)

1. El hotel es _____.

2. El estudiante es muy _____

3. El _____ no es difícil (*difficult*).

4. El museo es muy _____

5. Íñigo no es _____

■■■Pronunciación y ortografía • El alfabeto español

A. El alfabeto español. You will hear the names of the letters of the Spanish alphabet, along with a list of place names. Listen and repeat, imitating the speaker. Notice that most Spanish consonants are pronounced differently than in English. In future chapters, you will have the opportunity to practice the pronunciation of most of these letters individually.

a	a	la Argentina	ñ	eñe	España
b	be	Bolivia	o	o	Oviedo
c	ce	Cáceres	p	pe	Panamá
d	de	Durango	q	cu	Quito
e	e	el Ecuador	r	ere	el Perú
f	efe	Florida	rr	erre	Monterrey
g	ge	Guatemala	s	ese	San Juan
h	hache	Honduras	t	te	Toledo
i	i	Ibiza	u	u	el Uruguay
j	jota	Jalisco	v	ve	Venezuela
k	ca	(Kansas)	w	doble ve	(Washington)
l	ele	Lima	x	equis	Extremadura
m	eme	México	y	i griega	el Paraguay
n	ene	Nicaragua	z	zeta	Zaragoza

B. Repeticiones. Repeat the following words, phrases, and sentences. Imitate the speaker and pay close attention to the difference in pronunciation between Spanish and English.

1.	c/ch	Colón	Cecilia	Muchas gracias.	Buenas noches.
2.	g/gu	Ortega	gusto	Miguel	guitarra
3.	h	La Habana	Héctor	hotel	historia
4.	j/g	Jamaica	Jiménez	Geraldo	Gilda
5.	l/ll	Lupe	Manolo	Sevilla	me llamo
6.	y	Yolanda	yate	Paraguay	y
7.	r/rr	Mario	arte	Roberto	carro
8.	ñ	Begoña	Toño	señorita	Hasta mañana.

C. Más repeticiones. Repeat the following Spanish syllables, imitating the speaker. Try to pronounce each vowel with a short, tense sound.

1.	ma	fa	la	ta	pa
2.	me	fe	le	te	pe
3.	mi	fi	li	ti	pi
4.	mo	fo	lo	to	po
5.	mu	fu	lu	tu	pu
6.	sa	se	si	so	su

D. Las vocales. Compare the pronunciation of the following words in both English and Spanish. Listen for the schwa, the *uh* sound in English, and notice its absence in Spanish.

English: *banana*   Spanish: **banana**

        capital   **capital**

Now, repeat the following words, imitating the speaker. Be careful to avoid the English schwa. Remember to pronounce each vowel with a short and tense sound.

1. hasta	tal	nada	mañana	natural
2. me	qué	Pérez	usted	rebelde
3. sí	señorita	permiso	imposible	tímido
4. yo	con	cómo	noches	profesor
5. tú	uno	mucho	Perú	Lupe

E. ¿Español o inglés? You will hear a series of words. Each will be said twice. Circle the letter of the word you hear, either a Spanish word (**español**) or an English word (**inglés**). Note that Spanish vowels are short and tense; they are never drawn out with a *u* or *i* glide as in English.

	ESPAÑOL	INGLÉS
1.	a. mi	b. me
2.	a. fe	b. Fay
3.	a. es	b. ace
4.	a. con	b. cone
5.	a. ti	b. tea
6.	a. lo	b. low

F. Dictado

Paso 1. You will hear a series of words that are probably unfamiliar to you. Each will be said twice. Listen carefully, concentrating on the vowel sounds, and write in the missing vowels. (Check your answers in the Appendix.)

1. r____d____ll____

2. M____r____b____l

3. ____n____l____t____r____l

4. s____lv____v____d____s

5. ____lv____d____d____z____

Paso 2. Imagine that you work as a hotel receptionist in Miami. Listen to how some Hispanic guests spell out their last names for you. Write down the names as you hear them. (Check your answers in the Appendix.)

1. _____

2. _____

3. _____

4. _____

SEGUNDA PARTE

■■■Los números del 0 al 30; *Hay*

A. Canción infantil. You will hear a reading of the following children's song. It will be read with pauses for repetition. First, listen to the reading of the song.

Canción infantil

Dos y dos son cuatro,
cuatro y dos son seis,
seis y dos son ocho,
y ocho dieciséis.

B. ¿Cuánto es? (*How much does it cost?*) You will hear the price of three different brands of items you want to purchase in pesos (the unit of currency in many Hispanic countries). Repeat the price of the *least* expensive brand. In this exercise, you will practice listening for specific information. (Remember to repeat the correct answer.)

1. ... 2. ... 3. ... 4. ...

C. ¿Cuántos hay? (*How many are there?*) Read the following phrases when you hear the corresponding numbers. (Remember to repeat the correct answer.)

1. 21 personas (*f.*)
2. 18 profesores

3. 1 señora (*f.*)
4. 21 días (*m.*)
5. 30 cafés

D. ¿Qué hay en el salón de clase? (*What is there in the classroom?*) You will hear a series of questions. Each will be said twice. Answer based on the following drawing. (Remember to repeat the correct answer.)

1. ... 2. ... 3. ... 4. ...

■■■Los gustos y las preferencias (Part 1)

A. ¿Qué te gusta? (*What do you like?*)

Paso 1. You will hear a series of questions. For each question, check the appropriate answer. No answers will be given.

The answers you choose should be correct for you.

1. ☐ ¡Sí, me gusta!   ☐ ¡No, no me gusta!

2. ☐ ¡Sí, creo que (*I think*) es fantástico!   ☐ ¡No, no me gusta!

3. ☐ Sí, me gusta.   ☐ No, no me gusta.

4. ☐ Sí, me gusta.   ☐ No, no me gusta.

Paso 2. Interview Professor Morales about his likes and dislikes using the oral cues. Remember to use **¿Le gusta... ?** and to repeat the correct question. You will hear his answer.

> MODELO: (*you hear*) la universidad →
> (*you say*) ¿Le gusta la universidad?   (*you hear*) Sí, me gusta mucho.

1. ... 2. ... 3. ... 4. ...

B. Los gustos y las preferencias. You will hear a series of questions. Each will be said twice. You should be able to guess the meaning of the verbs based on context. Answer based on your own experience. You will hear a possible answer. (Remember to repeat the answer.)

> MODELO: (*you see*) jugar
> (*you hear*) ¿Te gusta jugar al tenis? →
> (*you say*) Sí, me gusta jugar al tenis. OR No, no me gusta jugar al tenis.

1. jugar   2. estudiar   3. tocar   4. comer

■■■Los hispanos hablan: ¿Qué tipo de música te gusta más?

> In this section of the Laboratory Manual, you will hear authentic passages from Hispanics about a variety of subjects, including their school experiences, food preferences, hobbies, and so on. As you listen, try not to be distracted by unfamiliar vocabulary. Concentrate instead on what you *do* know and understand.*

In addition to the types of music that most young people listen to here in the United States (soft rock, heavy metal, and so on), Hispanic students also listen to music that is typical of their own country or region. Have you heard of **la salsa, el merengue,** or **el tango?** These are all types of music from different regions of Spanish America. Note that the word **conjunto** means *musical group.*

You will hear a passage in which a student tells about her likes and dislikes in music. First, listen to get a general idea of the content. Then, go back and listen again for specific information. Then you will hear a series of statements. Circle **C (cierto)** if the statement is true or **F (falso)** if it is false.

Habla Teresa: Me gusta más el *rock* en inglés y en español. Mis cantantes favoritos son Sting y Whitney Houston. Mis conjuntos favoritos son Metálica y Hombres G, un conjunto que canta en español. Me gusta la música instrumental y me encanta la música latina por su ritmo y su sabor... y porque es nuestra. Me gustan la salsa y el merengue. Me gusta la música en inglés y español. ¡Amo toda la música!

1. C   F   2. C   F   3. C   F

■■■¿Qué hora es?

A. ¿Qué hora es?

Paso 1. You will hear a series of times. Each will be said twice. Circle the letter of the clock face that indicates the time you hear.

     MODELO: (*you hear*) Son las diez de la mañana. → (*you circle the letter a*)

  (a.)   b.

1. a.   b.

---

*The listening text for the **Los hispanos hablan** sections will appear in the Laboratory Manual through **Capítulo 2.**

2. a.    b.

3. a.    b.

4. a.    b.

Paso 2. Now when you hear a number, tell the time that you see on the corresponding clock. Repeat the correct answer.

MODELO: (*you see*) 1.

(*you hear*) uno →
(*you say*) Son las tres y media de la tarde.

2.    3.    4.   5.

B. ¿A qué hora es… ? You will hear a series of questions about Marisol's schedule. Answer based on her schedule. (Remember to repeat the correct answer.) First, pause and look at the schedule.

MODELO: (*you hear*) ¿A qué hora es la clase de español? →
(*you say*) Es a las ocho y media de la mañana.

Horario escolar*

Nombre: Marisol Abad
Dirección: Calle Alfaro, 16
Teléfono: 72-45-86

8:30	Español
9:40	Ciencias
11:00	Matemáticas
12:25	Inglés
2:15	Arte

*School schedule

---

1. …   2. …   3. …   4. …

UN POCO DE TODO | (Para entregar)*

A. En el periódico (*newspaper*). You will hear a series of headlines from a Spanish newspaper. Each will be said twice. Write the number of the headline next to the section of the newspaper in which it most likely appears. Try not to be distracted by unfamiliar vocabulary; concentrate instead on the key words in the headline. First, listen to the list of sections.

_____ Política

_____ Libros (*Books*)

_____ Espectáculos (*Entertainment*)

_____ Deportes (*Sports*)

_____ Economía

B. *Listening Passage:* ¿Qué idiomas se hablan en Latinoamérica?†

The first listening passage, as well as the passages in other chapters of the Laboratory Manual, will be preceded by prelistening exercises (**Antes de escuchar**). They will involve strategies such as predicting and guessing content before you listen, reading the true/false statements before listening, and so on. You should always do the prelistening section *before* you listen to the passage. Don't be distracted by unfamiliar vocabulary. Focus on what you *do* know. In most cases, you will be asked to listen for specific information.

---

*No answers are given for **Para entregar** activities.
†The text for the Listening Passages will appear in the Laboratory Manual through **Capítulo 2.**

Antes de escuchar (*Before listening*). Before you listen to the passage, pause and do the following prelistening exercises.

Paso 1. Read the true/false statements. As you read them, try to infer the information you will hear in the passage, as well as listen for specific information.

1. Julia es de México.
2. Tegucigalpa es la capital de Honduras.
3. Julia habla guaraní.
4. No se habla portugués en Latinoamérica.
5. Las palabras (*words*) **español** y **castellano** son sinónimas.
6. El español es la única (*only*) lengua que se habla en Latinoamérica.

Paso 2. What can you infer from the true/false statements? Check all that apply.

☐ Julia will probably tell us where she is from and what language she speaks.

☐ There may be more than one word to describe the Spanish language.

☐ It is possible that more than one language is spoken throughout Latin America.

Now resume listening.

Listening Passage. Now, you will hear a passage about the Spanish language and where it is spoken. First, listen to get a general idea of the content. Then, go back and listen again for specific information.

¡Hola! Me llamo Julia y soy de Tegucigalpa. ¡Sí! Tegucigalpa. ¿Es un nombre difícil? Tegucigalpa es la capital de Honduras. Honduras está en Centroamérica. En mi país se habla el castellano o español. **Español** y **castellano** son palabras sinónimas para hablar del mismo idioma. El castellano también se habla en España y en toda Latinoamérica. Bueno, no en toda Latinoamérica, porque en el Brasil se habla portugués y en Belice se habla inglés. Además del castellano, en el mundo hispánico se hablan otros idiomas también. Por ejemplo, en el Paraguay hay dos lenguas oficiales, el español y el guaraní. El guaraní es una lengua indígena original de la región. Mi amiga Susana es paraguaya y habla español y guaraní.

El español es una lengua muy importante en el mundo, porque lo hablan muchas personas. ¿Se habla español en tu estado?

Now pause and do the exercises in **Después de escuchar.**

Después de escuchar (*After listening*)

Paso 1. Here are the true/false statements. Circle **C** (**cierto**) if the statement is true or **F** (**falso**) if it is false. Then, correct the statements that are false, according to the passage.

1. C F Julia es de México.

   _____

2. C F Tegucigalpa es la capital de Honduras.

   _____

3. C F Julia habla guaraní.

   _____

4. C F No se habla portugués en Latinoamérica.

   _____

5. C F Las palabras (*words*) **español** y **castellano** son sinónimas.

_____

6. C F El español es la única (*only*) lengua que se habla en Latinoamérica.

_____

Paso 2. Go back and listen to the passage again. Then, pause and complete the following sentences with words chosen from the list.

castellano	lengua
español	paraguaya
inglés	

1. La palabra **idioma** es sinónimo de _____.

2. Julia es de Honduras: es **hondureña.** Susana es del Paraguay: es _____.

3. Susana habla guaraní y _____ (o _____).

4. En Belice se habla _____.

Now resume listening.

C. Dictado. You will hear a radio announcement that tells the times of this afternoon's programs. Listen carefully and, while listening, write the time of each program next to the name of the program. After you listen to the radio announcement, pause and write the type of program you think each is in English. First, listen to the names of the programs.

HORA	PROGRAMA	TIPO DE PROGRAMA
_____	Radionovela	_____
_____	Informe meteorológico	_____
_____	Visita con el veterinario	_____
_____	Tarde musical	_____
_____	Radionoticias	_____
_____	Programa del Dr. Rodríguez	_____

Now resume listening.

D. Y para terminar... Entrevista. You will hear a series of questions. Each will be said twice. Answer based on your own experience. Pause and write the answers.

1. _____

2. _____

3. _____

4. _____

5. _____

6. _____

7. _____

VIDEOTECA   Minidramas*

Paso 1. Saludos y expresiones de cortesía. In the following conversation, Diego González introduces himself to Professor Salazar. Diego's lines will be read with pauses for repetition. But first, listen.

DIEGO: Perdón. ¿Es usted el profesor Salazar?
PROFESOR: Sí, yo soy.
DIEGO: Buenas tardes. Me llamo Diego González. Soy el estudiante de la Universidad de California.
PROFESOR: Ah, sí. El estudiante de Los Ángeles. Mucho gusto.
DIEGO: Igualmente.
PROFESOR: ¡Bienvenido a México! Él es Antonio Sifuentes. Es estudiante posgraduado en la facultad.
ANTONIO: ¿Qué tal, Diego?
DIEGO: Muy bien, gracias. ¿Y tú?
ANTONIO: Muy bien. Mucho gusto.
DIEGO: Igualmente, Antonio.

Paso 2. Aplicación. Now you will participate in a similar conversation, partially printed in your manual, in which you will play the role of Mariana, an exchange student in Mexico. Complete the conversation using the written cues. (Remember to repeat the correct answer. If you wish, pause and write the answers.) Here are the cues for your conversation.

mucho gusto, Gabriel   muchas gracias   es fantástica

PABLO: Mariana, te presento a (*I'd like to introduce you to*) Gabriel Herrera, un estudiante posgraduado de la facultad.

MARIANA: _____

GABRIEL: El gusto es mío (*mine*). Bienvenida a México, Mariana.

MARIANA: _____

GABRIEL: ¿Qué tal te gusta la universidad?

MARIANA: Pues, ¡creo que (*I think that*) _____!

PRUEBA CORTA

Hablando (*Speaking*) **de las clases.** You will overhear a conversation between Geraldo and Delia. Listen carefully. Try not to be distracted by unfamiliar vocabulary; concentrate instead on what you do know. Then, you will hear a series of statements. Circle **C** (**cierto**) if the statement is true and **F** (**falso**) if it is false.

1. C   F   2. C   F   3. C   F   4. C   F   5. C   F

---

*This **Minidramas** videoclip is available on the DVD to accompany *Puntos de partida*, Eighth Edition.

CAPÍTULO **1**

VOCABULARIO Preparación

A. ¿Qué necesita? (*What does she need?*) Luisa is making a list of things that she will need for her classes this semester. Listen carefully to her list and check the items that she needs. If she mentions a number, write it in the space provided. Don't be distracted by unfamiliar vocabulary; concentrate instead on the words that you *do* know. ¡OJO! Not all items will be mentioned. First, listen to the list of possible items. (Check your answers in the Appendix.)

COSAS	SÍ	NO	¿CUÁNTOS O CUÁNTAS?
mochila(s)			
lápiz (lápices)			
bolígrafo(s)			
libro(s) de texto			
cuaderno(s)			
diccionario(s)			
calculadora(s)			
papel			
pizarra(s)			

B. Identificaciones. Identify the following items when you hear the corresponding number. Begin each sentence with **Es el...** or **Es la...** (Remember to repeat the correct answer.)

1. ... 2. ... 3. ... 4. ... 5. ... 6. ... 7. ... 8. ... 9. ... 10. ...

C. Preguntas y respuestas (*Questions and answers*). Imagine that your friend Marisa has just made some statements that you didn't quite understand. You will hear each statement twice. Circle the letter of the interrogative word or phrase you would use to obtain information about what she said.

1. a. ¿a qué hora?   b. ¿cómo es?
2. a. ¿quién?   b. ¿dónde?
3. a. ¿cuál?   b. ¿dónde está?
4. a. ¿cuántas?   b. ¿cuándo?
5. a. ¿qué es?   b. ¿cómo es?
6. a. ¿cómo está?   b. ¿qué es?

D. Dictado. You will hear five questions. Each will be said twice. Write each question next to the appropriate drawing. First, pause and look at the drawings. (Check your answers in the Appendix.)

1. _____

2. _____

3. _____

Nombre _____ Fecha _____ Clase _____

4. _____

5. _____

■■■Los hispanos hablan: ¿Qué materias te gusta estudiar?

You will hear three Hispanic students describe the courses they like or don't like. As you listen to each one, complete the following chart with **sí** or **no**. Use **sí** to indicate that the student likes a given subject, and **no** to indicate that he or she does not. You will hear the students in the order given in the chart. ¡OJO! The students may mention subjects other than those listed in the chart. (Check your answers in the Appendix.)

1. *Habla José:* Me gustan mucho la química, la física, la biología, la sicología y la literatura. ¡No me gustan para nada las matemáticas!
2. *Habla Raúl:* No me gustan los idiomas. Pienso que todo el mundo debería hablar el mismo idioma, el español, claro. Me gustan mucho las ciencias porque las entiendo bien.
3. *Habla Julia:* Me gustan las matemáticas y la sicología. Me gustan mucho los números y también me gusta saber lo que está pensando la gente. No me gustan la historia y la química. Realmente no me interesa el pasado y detesto las fórmulas y los laboratorios.

MATERIAS	1. JOSÉ	2. RAÚL	3. JULIA
Historia			
Matemáticas			
Sicología			
Química			
Física			
Biología			
Idiomas			
Ciencias			

PRONUNCIACIÓN Y ORTOGRAFÍA | Diphthongs and Linking

A. Repaso: Las vocales. Repeat the following words, imitating the speaker. Pay close attention to the pronunciation of the indicated vowels.

WEAK VOWELS

(i, y)	Pili	silla	soy	y
(u)	gusto	lugar	uno	mujer

STRONG VOWELS

(a)	calculadora	Ana	banana	lápiz
(e)	trece	papel	clase	general
(o)	profesor	hombre	Lola	bolígrafo

B. Diptongos. Diphthongs are formed by two successive weak vowels (**i** or **y, u**) or by a combination of a weak vowel and a strong vowel (**a, e, o**). The two vowels are pronounced as a single syllable. Repeat the following words, imitating the speaker. Pay close attention to the pronunciation of the indicated diphthongs.

1. (ia) **media** — gra**cias**
2. (ie) **bien** — s**ie**te
3. (io) **Julio** — edif**icio**
4. (iu) c**iu**dad (*city*) — v**iu**da (*widow*)
5. (ua) c**ua**derno — Mana**gua**
6. (ue) b**ue**nos — n**ue**ve
7. (ui) m**uy** — f**ui** (*I was / I went*)
8. (uo) c**uo**ta — ard**uo**
9. (ai) **ai**re — h**ay**
10. (ei) v**ei**nte — tr**ei**nta
11. (oi) s**oy** — est**oy**
12. (au) **au**to — p**au**sa
13. (eu) d**eu**da (*debt*) — C**eu**ta

C. Más sobre (*about*) **los diptongos**

Paso 1. Diphthongs can occur within a word or between words, causing the words to be "linked" and pronounced as one long word. Repeat the following phrases and sentences, imitating the speaker. Pay close attention to how the words are linked.

1. (oi/ia) Armando y Alicia
   las letras o y hache
2. (ei/ie) el tigre y el chimpancé
   Vicente y Elena
3. (oi/ie/ai/io) Soy extrovertida y optimista.
4. (ai/iu) Elena y Humberto necesitan una mochila y unos libros.

Paso 2. Linking also occurs naturally between many word boundaries in Spanish. Repeat the following sentences, imitating the speaker. Try to say each without pause, as if it were one long word.

1. ¿Es usted eficiente?
2. ¿Dónde hay un escritorio?
3. Tomás y Alicia están en la oficina.

4. Están en la Argentina y en el Uruguay.

5. No hay estudiantes en el edificio a estas horas (*at these hours*).

D. Dictado. You will hear a series of words containing diphthongs. Each will be said twice. Listen carefully and write the missing vowels. (Check your answers in the Appendix.)

1. c_____nc_____s

2. Patric_____

3. s_____s

4. b_____nos

5. _____to

6. s_____

GRAMÁTICA

1. Identifying People, Places, Things, and Ideas (Part 1) • Singular Nouns: Gender and Articles

A. Gramática en acción: La lista de José María. You will hear the list of supplies and texts that José María needs for two of his classes. As you listen, complete the following chart by checking the items you hear for each class. Be careful, as not all items from the list will be in the chart, and the items in the chart are not in order! (Check your answers in the Appendix.)

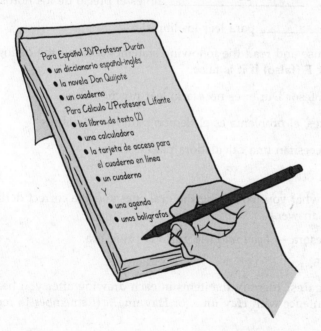

Para Español 30/Profesor Durán
- un diccionario español-inglés
- la novela Don Quijote
- un cuaderno

Para Cálculo 2/Profesora Lifante
- los libros de texto (2)
- una calculadora
- la tarjeta de acceso para el cuaderno en línea
- un cuaderno

Y
- una agenda
- unos bolígrafos

	ESPAÑOL 30	CÁLCULO 2
un cuaderno		
un diccionario español-inglés		
una calculadora		
los libros de texto		
la novela *Don Quijote*		
la tarjeta de acceso para el cuaderno en línea		

B. En la clase del profesor Durán: El primer día

Paso 1. Dictado. The dialogue below will be read twice. Listen carefully the first time; the second time, write in the missing words. (Check your answers in the Appendix).

PROFESOR DURÁN: Aquí está _____

_____ del curso.

Son necesarios _____

_____ de texto y

_____ diccionario. También hay

_____ _____

de _____ y libros

de poesía.

ESTUDIANTE 1:   ¡Es una lista infinita!

ESTUDIANTE 2:   Sí, y los libros cuestan demasiado.

ESTUDIANTE 1:   No, _____ _____ no es el precio de los libros. ¡Es _____

_____ para leer los libros!

Paso 2. ¿Cierto o falso? Now pause and read the following statements about the dialogue. Circle **C** (**cierto**) if the statement is true or **F** (**falso**) if it is false.

1. C   F   En la clase del profesor Durán es necesario leer muchos libros.

2. C   F   Para los estudiantes, el problema es el tiempo para leer los libros.

3. C   F   Los estudiantes necesitan una calculadora para la clase.

Now resume listening.

C. ¿Qué te gusta? Tell a friend what you like, using the oral cues and the correct definite article. (Remember to repeat the correct answer.)

MODELO: (*you hear*) profesora → (*you say*) Me gusta la profesora.

1. ...   2. ...   3. ...   4. ...   5. ...

D. ¿Qué hay en estos (*these*) lugares? Identify the items in each drawing after you hear the corresponding number. Begin each sentence with **Hay un...** or **Hay una...** (Remember to repeat the correct answer.)

MODELO: (*you see*) diccionario → (*you say*) Hay un diccionario en la mesa.

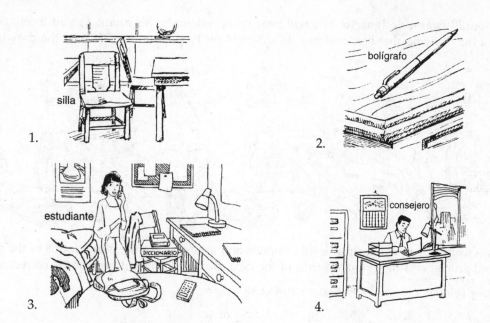

1.

2.

3.

4.

2. Identifying People, Places, Things, and Ideas (Part 2) • Nouns and Articles: Plural Forms

A. Gramática en acción: Un anuncio

Paso 1. You will hear the following ad. Listen carefully and read along with the speakers. Do not be distracted by unfamiliar vocabulary. Focus instead on the words that you do know.

Paso 2. Pause and complete the following sentences based on the preceding ad. (Check your answers in the Appendix.)

1. The plural of **curso** is _____.

2. The plural of **idioma** is _____.

3. The plural of **universidad** is _____.

4. To express **residential program** in Spanish, you would say _____.

Now resume listening.

B. Descripción: El cuarto de Ignacio. You will hear Ignacio describe his room. As you listen, circle the number of the drawing that best matches his description. First, pause and look at the drawings.

1. 2. 3.

C. Cambios (*Changes*). You will hear a series of nouns and articles. Give the plural forms of the first four nouns and articles and the singular forms of the next four. (Remember to repeat the correct answer.)

SINGULAR → PLURAL   PLURAL → SINGULAR

1. ... 2. ... 3. ... 4. ...   5. ... 6. ... 7. ... 8. ...

D. Los errores de Inés. You will hear some statements that your friend Inés makes about the following drawing. She is wrong and you must correct her. (Remember to repeat the correct answer.)

MODELO: (*you hear*) Hay dos libros. → (*you say*) No. Hay tres libros.

1. ... 2. ... 3. ... 4. ... 5. ... 6. ...

E. Dictado. You will hear a series of sentences. Each will be said twice. Listen carefully and write the missing words. You will be listening for words that are either singular or plural. (Check your answers in the Appendix.)

1. Hay _____ _____ en _____ _____.

2. _____ _____ _____ están en _____ _____.

3. No hay _____ _____ en _____ _____.

4. ¿Hay _____ _____ en _____ _____?

3. Expressing Actions • Subject Pronouns (Part 1); Present Tense of *-ar* Verbs; Negation

A. Gramática en acción: Una escena en la biblioteca. You will hear a description of the following drawing. After listening, pause and read each statement about the description. Circle **C (cierto)** if the statement is true or **F (falso)** if it is false. If the information is not contained in or cannot be inferred from the description, circle **ND (No lo dice** [*It doesn't say*]). In this exercise, you will be listening for specific information.

1.   C   F   ND   Cuatro estudiantes trabajan hoy en esta (*this*) sección de la biblioteca.

2.   C   F   ND   El narrador (*The narrator*) trabaja en la biblioteca.

3.   C   F   ND   Manuel y el narrador estudian para un examen de matemáticas.

4.   C   F   ND   El amigo del profesor (*The professor's friend*) trabaja en la biblioteca.

B.   ¿Quién habla? You will hear a series of sentences. Each will be said twice. Listen carefully and circle the letter of the *subject* of each sentence. In this exercise, you will practice listening for specific information.

1.   a.   yo   b.   ella
2.   a.   él   b.   tú
3.   a.   Ana y yo   b.   los estudiantes
4.   a.   Alberto   b.   Alberto y tú
5.   a.   Uds.   b.   nosotras

C.   ¿Quién... ? Answer the following questions using the oral cues. (Remember to repeat the correct answer.)

1.   ¿Quién canta bien?

   MODELO: (*you hear*) Juan → (*you say*) Juan canta bien.

   a. ...   b. ...   c. ...   d. ...

2.   ¿Quién practica deportes (*sports*)?

   MODELO: (*you hear*) yo → (*you say*) Yo practico deportes.

   a. ...   b. ...   c. ...   d. ...

D.   Mis compañeros y yo. Form complete sentences about yourself and others, using the oral and written cues. (Remember to repeat the correct answer.)

   MODELO: (*you see and hear*) yo   (*you hear*) pagar la matrícula →
             (*you say*) Pago la matrícula.

1.   Ana y yo
2.   Chela y Roberto
3.   el estudiante de Chile
4.   Jaime, tú...
5.   profesor, Ud. ...

E. ¿Dónde están?

Paso 1. Look at the drawings. Tell where the people might be when you hear the corresponding question. (Remember to repeat the correct answer.)

MODELO: (*you hear*) ¿Dónde está Alicia? →
(*you say*) Está en el salón de clase.

Paso 2. Now pause and write what each person might be doing at each location. (Check the Appendix for possible answers.)

Now resume listening.

4. Getting Information • Asking Yes/No Questions

A. Gramática en acción: La oficina de matrículas. You will hear a dialogue. After listening, read the series of statements. Circle the letter of the person who might have made each statement. In this exercise, you will practice listening for specific information.

a. la estudiante   b. el consejero

1. a. b. No deseo tomar una clase por la noche.

2. a. b. ¿Qué tal el Francés 10?

3. a. b. ¿Hay sitio en la clase de Sicología 2?

Now resume listening.

B. ¿Es una pregunta? You will hear a series of statements and questions. Listen carefully and circle the appropriate letter. Pay close attention to intonation.

1. a. statement   b. question   4. a. statement   b. question
2. a. statement   b. question   5. a. statement   b. question
3. a. statement   b. question

C. Entrevista con la profesora Villegas

Paso 1. Interview Professor Villegas for your school newspaper, using the following cues. Use the **Ud.** form of the verbs. Use the subject pronoun **Ud.** in your first question only. Professor Villegas will answer your questions. (Remember to repeat the correct question.)

MODELO: (*you see and hear*) enseñar / inglés →
(*you say*) ¿Enseña Ud. inglés?   (*you hear*) No, enseño español.

1. enseñar / cuatro clases   4. hablar / con los estudiantes
2. enseñar / francés   5. le gusta / la universidad
3. trabajar / por la noche

Paso 2. ¿Qué recuerda Ud.? (*What do you remember?*) Now pause and report what Professor Villegas said about herself. Use **La profesora Villegas...** in your first sentence only. (Check the Appendix for possible answers.)

MODELO: La profesora Villegas enseña español.

1. _____

2. _____

3. _____

4. _____

5. _____

Now resume listening.

A. Un día en la vida (*life*) de Armando

Paso 1. You will hear a series of sentences that describe a typical day in Armando's life. Each will be said twice. Listen carefully and circle the letter of the drawing that best matches each sentence. First, pause and look at the drawings.

1. a.

b.

2. a.

b.

3. a.

b.

4. a.

b.

---

*No answers are given for **Para entregar** activities.

Paso 2. ¿Qué recuerda Ud.? (*What do you remember?*) Now pause and write sentences that describe the actions in the drawings you chose.

1. _____

2. _____

3. _____

4. _____

Now resume listening.

B. *Listening Passage:* **¿Cómo son las universidades hispánicas?**

Antes de escuchar. Before you listen to the passage, pause and do the following prelistening exercises.

Paso 1. The passage contains some general information about Hispanic universities and how they differ from universities in the United States. Check the specific information that you expect to find in the passage.

☐ how the academic year is divided (that is, into semesters, quarters, and so on)

☐ the number of courses or credits that students are required to take

☐ the length of the academic year

☐ how much professors are paid

☐ how soon students need to declare their major

☐ whether or not foreign students attend Hispanic universities

Paso 2. The passage also contains information about Julia's course of studies. What information do you think she will give you?

☐ her major   ☐ which courses she has to take for her major

☐ which professors she likes best   ☐ the name of the university she attends

Now resume listening.

Listening Passage. Now you will hear a passage about Hispanic universities. In this passage, Julia talks about her major, **su especialización,** and some of the differences between Hispanic and U.S. universities.

¡Hola! ¿Qué tal? Soy tu amiga Julia, la hondureña. Estudio en la Universidad de Salamanca, en España. Mi carrera es ciencias políticas. La carrera es la especialización académica, como *major* o concentración.

En el mundo hispánico las universidades son muy diferentes de las de los Estados Unidos. Por lo general, no hay semestres. El año académico dura nueve meses. Los estudiantes toman de cuatro a siete cursos en un año. Además, los estudiantes no esperan dos años para declarar su carrera o especialización.

Yo tomo muchos cursos en relación con las ciencias políticas. ¿Cuáles? Pues, cursos de historia, filosofía, economía, estadística, etcétera. También tomo inglés. Estudio mucho, porque, como en todas las universidades, es necesario estudiar mucho en las universidades de España para pasar los cursos.

A pesar de eso, me gusta la vida universitaria. En Salamanca hay muchos estudiantes extranjeros, y muchos son de los Estados Unidos, como mi amiga Heather, que es de Carolina del Norte. Nosotras practicamos el español y el inglés muchas tardes después de las clases. ¿Con quién practicas tú el español?

Después de escuchar. Go back and listen to the passage again. Then, pause and complete the following sentences with words chosen from the list.

el alemán	ciencias naturales	especialización	el inglés
carrera	ciencias políticas	extranjeros	semestres

1. Para expresar el concepto de *major*, se usa la palabra _____

   (o _____) en español.

2. Por lo general, no hay _____ en el año académico hispánico.

3. Julia toma cursos en relación con las _____

4. También toma una lengua extranjera: _____.

5. En Salamanca, hay muchos estudiantes _____

Now resume listening.

C. Y para terminar… Entrevista. You will hear a series of questions about your classes and your life at the university. Each will be said twice. Answer based on your own experience. Pause and write the answers.

Note: The word **tu** means *your*, and **mi** means *my*.

1. _____
2. _____
3. _____
4. _____
5. _____
6. _____

VIDEOTECA   Minidramas*

Paso 1. Gustos y preferencias. In the following conversation, Diego and Lupe discover that they have certain things in common. Lupe's lines will be read with pauses for repetition. But first, listen.

DIEGO: ¡Ay, perdón!
LUPE: No hay por qué. ¡Ay, Diego!
DIEGO: ¡Lupe! ¿Qué haces?
LUPE: Busco un libro para la clase de antropología.
DIEGO: ¿Te gusta la antropología?
LUPE: Sí, me gusta mucho. Sobre todo, me gusta la antropología precolombina.
DIEGO: ¿En serio? Es mi materia favorita. ¿Qué clase tomas?
LUPE: Tomo la clase del profesor Salazar. Es una clase fascinante.
DIEGO: Yo también tomo esa clase. Así que somos compañeros… Bueno, Lupe, nos vemos en clase.
LUPE: Sí, nos vemos.

_____
*This **Minidramas** videoclip is available on the DVD to accompany *Puntos de partida*, Eighth Edition.

Paso 2. Aplicación. Now you will participate in a similar conversation, partially printed in your manual, in which you play the role of Héctor. Complete the conversation using the written cues. (Remember to repeat the correct answer. If you wish, pause and write the answers.) Here are the cues for your conversation.

hola, Laura   dos libros más   profesor Serrano   a las 8:30 de la noche

HÉCTOR: ¡_____!

LAURA: ¿Qué tal, Héctor? ¿Qué buscas?

HÉCTOR: Pues, necesito _____ para la clase del

_____.

LAURA: Ah, sí... Es una clase fascinante, pero es necesario comprar muchos libros. A propósito (*By the way*), ¿a qué hora deseas estudiar en la biblioteca?

HÉCTOR: ¿Qué tal _____?

LAURA: ¡De acuerdo!

PRUEBA CORTA

Cosas de todos los días

Paso 1. Practice talking about your university, using the written cues. When you hear the corresponding number, form sentences using the words provided in the order given, making any necessary changes or additions. (Remember to repeat the correct answer.)

MODELO: (*you see*) 1. profesores / llegar / temprano / a / universidad   (*you hear*) uno →
(*you say*) *Los* profesores *llegan* temprano a *la* universidad.

2. consejeros / trabajar / en / oficina
3. mi amiga y yo / estudiar / en / biblioteca
4. en clase / nosotros / escuchar / a / profesores
5. fin de semana / mis amigos y yo / bailar / en / discoteca
6. por la mañana / (yo) / practicar / vocabulario
7. por la noche / (yo) / mirar / televisión

Paso 2. ¿Qué recuerda Ud.? Now you will hear a series of questions. Each will be said twice. Answer based on the preceding sentences. If you prefer, pause and write the answers. (Remember to repeat the correct answer.)

1. _____
2. _____
3. _____
4. _____

CAPÍTULO 2

VOCABULARIO   Preparación

A. Definiciones. You will hear a series of definitions of family relationships. Each will be said twice. Listen carefully and write the number of the definition next to the word defined. First, listen to the list of words.

_____ mi (*my*) abuelo   _____ mi hermano   _____ mi tío

_____ mi tía   _____ mi prima   _____ mi abuela

B. La familia Muñoz. You will hear a brief description of Sarita Muñoz's family. Listen carefully and complete the following family tree according to the description. First, pause and look at the family tree. (Check your answers in the Appendix.)

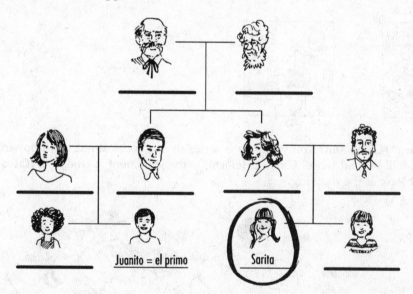

Juanito = el primo   Sarita

C. Dictado: El inventario. Imagine that you and a friend, Isabel, are taking inventory at the university bookstore where you work. Write out the numerals as she dictates the list to you. She will say each number twice. ¡OJO! Items are given in random order. First, listen to the list of words. (Check your answers in the Appendix.)

_____ mochilas

_____ lápices

_____ cuadernos

_____ novelas

_____ calculadoras

_____ libros de español

D. ¿Cuál es? You will hear a series of descriptions. Each will be said twice. Circle the letter of the item or person described.

1. a.   b.   2. a.   b.

3. a.   b.   4. a.   b.

5. a.   b.

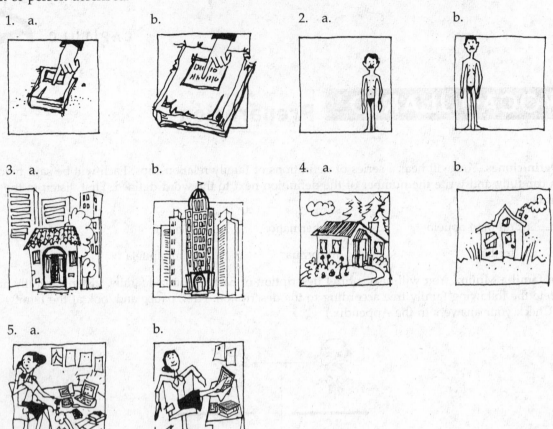

E. Descripciones: ¿Cómo son? You will hear a series of sentences about the following fathers and their sons. Each will be said twice. Circle **C** (**cierto**) if the statement is true or **F** (**falso**) if it is false. First, pause and look at the drawing.

1. C F   2. C F   3. C F   4. C F

■■■Los hispanos hablan: Dinos algo acerca de (*Tell us something about*) tu familia*

You will hear the following passage in which a student tells you about his family. Then you will hear a series of statements. Circle **C** (**cierto**) if the statement is true or **F** (**falso**) if it is false. If the information is not contained in the passage, circle **ND** (**No lo dice**).

Habla Antonio: Me llamo Antonio y soy de España. Ahora estudio en los Estados Unidos. Tengo tres hermanos que estudian aquí también, dos hermanos y una hermana. Tengo diecisiete años. En cuanto a los gustos, los cuatro somos un poco diferentes. A mí me gusta practicar deportes; a mi hermana le gusta cantar; a uno de mis hermanos le encanta escuchar música y al otro hermano le gusta mucho mirar deportes en la televisión. Físicamente somos muy similares, aunque creo que algunos vamos a ser más altos que otros. En cuanto a la personalidad, somos muy diferentes. Por ejemplo, yo soy una persona muy introvertida y pacífica. Sin embargo, mi hermana es muy extrovertida y gregaria.

1. C F ND   2. C F ND   3. C F ND   4. C F ND

PRONUNCIACIÓN Y ORTOGRAFÍA — Stress and Written Accent Marks (Part 1)

A. Repeticiones. Repeat the following words, imitating the speaker. The highlighted syllable receives the stress in pronunciation.

1. If a word ends in a vowel, **n,** or **s,** stress normally falls on the next-to-the-last syllable.

   sin**ce**ra   inte**re**sante   cua**der**nos   e**xa**men

2. If a word ends in any other consonant, stress normally falls on the last syllable.

   es**tar**   libe**ral**   profe**sor**   pa**pel**

B. Más repeticiones. Repeat the following words, imitating the speaker. The words have been divided into syllables for you. Pay close attention to which syllable receives the spoken stress.

1. Stress on the next-to-the-last syllable

li-bro	si-lla	cla-se	me-sa	Car-men
con-se-je-ra	li-te-ra-tu-ra	o-ri-gen	com-pu-ta-do-ra	cien-cias

2. Stress on the last syllable

se-ñor	mu-jer	fa-vor	ac-tor	co-lor
po-pu-lar	li-ber-tad	ge-ne-ral	sen-ti-men-tal	u-ni-ver-si-dad

C. Dictado. You will hear the following words. Each will be said twice. Listen carefully and circle the syllable that receives the spoken stress. (Check your answers in the Appendix.)

1. con-trol
2. e-le-fan-te
3. mo-nu-men-tal
4. com-pa-ñe-ra
5. bue-nos
6. us-ted

---

*This is the last **Los hispanos hablan** section to include a transcript of the spoken text in the Laboratory Manual.

GRAMÁTICA

5. Describing • Adjectives: Gender, Number, and Position

A. Gramática en acción: Un poema sencillo

Paso 1. You will hear the following poem. Listen carefully and read along with the speakers, Marta and Mario.

Amigo		Amiga
Fiel		Fiel
Amable		Amable
Simpático		Simpática
¡Lo admiro!		¡La admiro!

Paso 2. Now pause and check the adjectives that can be used to describe each person without making any changes to the adjectives. (Check your answers in the Appendix.)

	FIEL	AMABLE	SIMPÁTICO	SIMPÁTICA
Marta				
Mario				

Now resume listening.

B. Hablando (*Speaking*) de la familia. Imagine that your friend Graciela is describing her family. Listen to her description and check the adjectives that apply to each member of her family. ¡OJO! Not all the adjectives will be used, and not all adjectives in the description appear in the chart. In this exercise, you will practice listening for specific information. (Check your answers in the Appendix.)

	ACTIVOS	BAJO	ALTAS	JÓVENES	SOLTERO	CASADA
su tío						
los abuelos						
sus primos						
su hermana						
su padre						

C. ¿Cómo son? Practice describing various people, using the oral and written cues. Remember to change the endings of the adjectives if necessary. (Remember to repeat the correct answer.)

> MODELO: (*you see and hear*) mi profesora (*you hear*) lista →
> (*you say*) Mi profesora es lista.

1. mi compañero de cuarto
2. la profesora de español
3. Bernardo
4. Amanda
5. yo (*f.*)

D. ¿Qué dicen (*are saying*) estas personas? When you hear the corresponding number, tell what these people are saying. Use definite articles and appropriate adjectives from the list to modify the nouns in the drawings. First, listen to the list of adjectives. (Remember to repeat the correct answer.)

> alto   corto   grande   moreno   pequeño

1.

libro

2.

edificio

3.

lápiz

4.

niña

5.

silla

E. ¿De dónde son (*are*) y qué idioma hablan? Imagine that your friend Carmen is asking you about some of the exchange students on campus. You will hear each of her questions twice. Answer according to the model, giving the nationality of the persons she mentions and the language they might speak. First, listen to the list of nationalities. You will need to change the endings in some cases. (Remember to repeat the correct answer.)

> alemán   español   francés   inglés   italiano   portugués

> MODELO: (*you hear*) ¿Evaristo es de Portugal? → (*you say*) Sí, es portugués y habla portugués.

1. … 2. … 3. … 4. … 5. …

6. Expressing *to be* • Present Tense of *ser*; Summary of Uses (Part 2)

A. Gramática en acción: Presentaciones (*Introductions*)

Paso 1. You will hear a brief passage about Francisco Durán and his wife, Lola Benítez. As you listen, try not to be distracted by unfamiliar vocabulary. Concentrate instead on what you *do* know and understand. You may want to take notes on the information in the passage.

_____

_____

_____

Paso 2. ¿Qué recuerda Ud.? Now pause and complete the following sentences based on the passage and your notes. ¡OJO! Use a form of the verb **ser** in the first blank of each sentence. (Check your answers in the Appendix.)

1. Marta _____ la _____ de Lola y Francisco.

2. Lola _____ _____.

3. Lola y Francisco _____ de _____.

4. Lola _____ _____; Francisco es _____ y moreno.

Now resume listening.

B. ¿De dónde son? Practice telling where you and your imaginary family and friends are from, using the written cues. (Remember to repeat the correct answer.)

> MODELO: (*you see and hear*) mi amigo Aristides / Colombia →
> (*you say*) Mi amigo Aristides es de Colombia.

1. mi amigo Lorenzo / la Argentina
2. tú / Costa Rica
3. mis abuelos / Cuba
4. mi hermano y yo / Chile

C. ¿De quién son estas cosas? Imagine that your friend wants to know to whom certain items belong. Answer her questions using the written cues. ¡OJO! Don't forget that **de** + **el** form the contraction **del.** (Remember to repeat the correct answer.)

> MODELO: (*you hear*) ¿De quién es el escritorio? (*you see*) el cliente →
> (*you say*) Es del cliente.

1. el estudiante
2. la profesora
3. las secretarias
4. el Sr. Costas

D. ¿Para quién son los regalos? Imagine that you need to give gifts to several of your friends and relatives, and money is no object! You will hear the name and a brief description of each person. Each statement will be said twice. Select appropriate gifts for them from the following list. First, listen to the list. (Remember to repeat the correct answer.)

la calculadora   los CDs de Enrique Iglesias   las novelas románticas

los libros de filosofía   el coche nuevo

Use the phrases **para ella, para él,** and **para ellos,** as in the model.

> MODELO: (*you hear*) Tu (*Your*) hermano Juan es estudiante universitario. →
> (*you say*) Los libros de filosofía son para él.

1. ...   2. ...   3. ...   4. ...

7. Expressing Possession • (Unstressed) Possessive Adjectives (Part 1)

A. Gramática en acción: Invitación y posesión

Paso 1. You will hear three captions. Write the number of each caption under the correct drawing. Careful! There is an extra caption.

a. _____   b. _____

Paso 2. Now you will hear a series of statements. Each will be said twice. Circle **C** (**cierto**) if the statement is true or **F** (**falso**) if it is false.

   1. C   F   2. C   F   3. C   F   4. C   F

B. ¿Cómo es la familia de Vicente? Tell what Vicente's family is like, using the written cues and the correct form of the possessive adjective **su.** Say the sentence when you hear the corresponding number. ¡OJO! Watch for singular or plural forms of the verb **ser.** (Remember to repeat the correct answer.)

> MODELO: (*you see*) 1. tíos / bajos   (*you hear*) uno →
> (*you say*) Sus tíos son bajos.

2. tías / simpáticas
3. primos / altos
4. abuela / delgada

5. hermanos / mayores
6. madre / bonita

C. ¿Cómo es su universidad? Describe your university to an exchange student who has recently arrived on campus, using the written cues and the appropriate form of **nuestro** and the verb **ser.** Say the sentence when you hear the corresponding number. (Remember to repeat the correct answer.)

> MODELO: (*you see*) 1. universidad / vieja   (*you hear*) uno →
> (*you say*) Nuestra universidad es vieja.

2. profesores / buenos
3. clases / pequeñas
4. biblioteca / grande

5. consejeros / amables
6. estudiantes / buenos

8. Expressing Actions • Present Tense of *-er* and *-ir* Verbs; Subject Pronouns (Part 2)

A. Gramática en acción: Un estudiante típico

Paso 1. Dictado. You will hear the following paragraph in which Samuel introduces himself. Listen carefully and write in the missing words. (Check your answers in the Appendix before you begin **Paso 2.**)

Hola. Me llamo Samuel Flores Toledo. Soy estudiante y _____¹ a la Universidad

Nacional Autónoma de México. _____² con mi familia en la Ciudad de México.

_____³ pizza con frecuencia y _____⁴ cerveza en las fiestas.

_____⁵ muchos libros de antropología para mi especialización. También

_____⁶ muchas cartas a mi familia. _____⁷ que una educación

universitaria es muy importante. Por eso estudio y _____⁸ mucho. ¡Pero

_____⁹ también que es muy importante estar con los amigos y con la familia!

Paso 2. ¿Qué recuerda Ud.? Now pause and complete the following sentences based on the information in the passage. (Check your answers in the Appendix.)

1. Diego _____ a la Universidad Nacional Autónoma de México.

2. Él _____ con su familia.

3. Diego _____ pizza con frecuencia y _____ cerveza en las fiestas.

4. Él _____ muchos libros de antropología.

Now resume listening.

B. Un sábado típico de la familia Robles. Describe what happens on a typical Saturday at the Robles household, using the written and oral cues. Remember that subject pronouns are not always used in Spanish. (Remember to repeat the correct answer.)

    MODELO: (*you hear*) nosotros (*you see*) estar en casa → (*you say*) Estamos en casa.

1. leer el periódico
2. escribir cartas
3. asistir a un partido (*game*) de fútbol
4. abrir una carta de mi prima
5. comer a las seis

C. ¿Qué hacen? (*What are they doing?*) You will hear a series of statements describing actions. Each will be said twice. Write the number of the statement next to the drawing that matches the action described in each statement. First, pause and look at the drawings.

{

}

a. _____

b. _____

c. _____

d. _____

e. _____

f. _____

D. ¿Quién... ? Answer the following questions using the oral cues. Use subject pronouns only if necessary. (Remember to repeat the correct answer.)

1. ¿Quién come en la cafetería?

MODELO: (*you hear*) Evita → (*you say*) Evita come en la cafetería.

a. ... b. ... c. ... d. ...

2. ¿Quién vive en una residencia?

MODELO: (*you hear*) yo → (*you say*) Vivo en una residencia.

a. ... b. ... c. ... d. ...

A. ¿Cuál es la foto? You will hear a description of a photograph. Listen carefully and choose the photograph that is described. First, listen to the following new words that you will hear in the description.

el pelo	*hair*	el jardín	*garden*	prefiere	*he/she prefers*
negro	*black*	blanco	*white*		

Now pause and look at the photos.

1.

2.

3.

B. *Listening Passage:* **Las familias hispanas***

Antes de escuchar. Before you listen to the passage, pause and do the following prelistening exercises.

Paso 1. Read the following true/false statements. As you read them, try to infer the information the passage will give you, as well as the specific information for which you need to listen.

1. En las familias hispanas, más de (*more than*) dos generaciones viven en una sola casa.
2. Los abuelos no participan activamente en el cuidado (*care*) de los nietos.
3. Por lo general, las personas viejas viven en asilos (*nursing homes*).
4. Los abuelos cuidan (*care for*) a los nietos mientras (*while*) los padres trabajan.
5. Los hijos y los nietos cuidan a sus padres o a sus abuelos cuando estos (*the latter*) están viejos o enfermos.

---

*This is the last Listening Passage section to include a transcript of the spoken text in the Laboratory Manual.

Paso 2. The passage contains information about Julia's family and about Hispanic families in general. Which statements do you think apply to the Hispanic family in general?

☐ The Hispanic family is typically smaller than a U.S. family.

☐ Many Hispanic families are extended families; that is, more than one generation live in the same household.

☐ The elderly and the sick are often sent to nursing homes.

☐ Grandparents are important in the daily lives of families.

☐ Many young couples live with their in-laws until they can become independent.

Now resume listening.

Listening Passage. Now you will hear a passage about Hispanic families. In this passage, Julia talks about Hispanic families in general and about her own family in particular. The following words and phrases appear in the passage.

estadounidenses	de los Estados Unidos
No sólo... sino que además	*Not only . . . but also*
las ventajas	*advantages*
se ayudan	*they help each other*
el cuidado	*care*
enfermas	*sick*
murió	*he died*
la cuidamos	*we take care of her*

Here is the passage. First, listen to it to get a general idea of the content. Then go back and listen again for specific information.

Las familias hispanas son más grandes que las familias estadounidenses, por lo general. No sólo es normal tener más hijos, sino que además, con frecuencia los abuelos viven con la familia.

En español existe un nombre específico para los padres del esposo o esposa. Son los **suegros,** el suegro y la suegra. A veces si un matrimonio joven no tiene mucho dinero, los nuevos esposos viven con los padres de uno de ellos (o sea, los suegros).

Para muchos norteamericanos esta es una situación extraña, ¿no? Pero es una situación que tiene sus ventajas también. Las familias hispanas conservan un contacto muy fuerte entre varias generaciones. Los miembros de la familia se visitan mucho y se ayudan constantemente con el cuidado de los niños y el de las personas viejas o enfermas.

Como ejemplo, yo puedo hablar de mi familia. Mi abuela materna vive con mi familia, porque su esposo, mi abuelo Rafael, murió joven. Sólo tenía 60 años. Mi abuela siempre ayudó a mi mamá con nosotros, sus nietos. Y ahora que mi abuela está vieja, mi mamá y nosotros la cuidamos. Es ley de la vida, ¿no? Mi abuela está contenta porque ahora también puede pasar tiempo con sus bisnietos, los hijos de mi hermano.

Now pause and do the **Después de escuchar** exercises.

Después de escuchar

Paso 1. Here are the true/false statements. Circle **C** (**cierto**) if the statement is true or **F** (**falso**) if it is false. Then correct the statements that are false, according to the passage.

1. C F En las familias hispanas, más de dos generaciones viven en una sola casa.

   _____

2. C F Los abuelos no participan activamente en el cuidado de los nietos.

   _____

3. C F Por lo general, las personas viejas viven en asilos.

   _____

4. C F Los abuelos cuidan a los nietos mientras los padres trabajan.

   _____

5. C F Los hijos y los nietos cuidan a sus padres o a sus abuelos cuando estos están viejos o enfermos.

   _____

Paso 2. Go back and listen to the passage again. Then, pause and complete the following sentences with words chosen from the list.

bisnietos   grandes   materna   suegros

1. La madre de mi madre es mi abuela _____.

2. Mis _____ son los padres de mi esposo/a.

3. Los _____ son los hijos de los nietos.

4. Por lo general, las familias hispanas son más _____ que las familias estadounidenses.

Now resume listening.

C. Y para terminar… Entrevista. You will hear a series of questions. Each will be said twice. Answer based on your experience. Pause and write the answers.

1. _____

2. _____

3. _____

4. _____

5. _____

6. _____

7. _____

VIDEOTECA — Minidramas*

Paso 1. Presentaciones. In the following conversation, Paloma introduces her boyfriend, Gustavo, to her aunt. Paloma's lines will be read with pauses for repetition. But first, listen.

PALOMA: ¡Buenas tardes, tía Elisa!
ELISA: ¡Hola! ¡Adelante!
PALOMA: Tía, quiero presentarte a mi novio, Gustavo. Gustavo, esta es mi tía, Elisa Velasco.
GUSTAVO: Mucho gusto en conocerla, señora.
ELISA: El gusto es mío, Gustavo.
PALOMA: Y ya conoces a mi primo José Miguel.
JOSÉ MIGUEL: ¿Qué tal?
GUSTAVO: ¡Hola!

Paso 2. Aplicación. Now you will participate in a similar conversation, partially printed in your manual, in which you play the role of Gema. Complete the conversation, using the written cues. (Remember to repeat the correct answer. If you wish, you may pause and write the answers.) Here are the cues for your conversation.

bien, gracias   quiero presentarte   es estudiante en la facultad

PAULA: ¡Hola, Gema! ¿Cómo estás?

GEMA: _____. Tía, _____ a mi amiga Margarita. Ella

_____. Margarita, esta es mi tía, Paula Valverde.

PAULA: Mucho gusto, Margarita.

MARGARITA: El gusto es mío, Sra. Valverde.

PRUEBA CORTA

A. La familia de doña Isabel. You will hear a passage about doña Isabel's family. Read the passage along with the speaker and circle the numbers you hear.

¡La familia de doña Isabel es muy grande y extendida! Ella tiene **30 / 20** nietos en total, y **16 / 26** bisnietos (*great-grandchildren*). Doña Isabel tiene **89 / 99** años. Su hijo mayor, Diego, tiene **67 / 77** años. Su hija menor, Alida, tiene **64 / 54**. Doña Isabel tiene **10 / 6** hijos en total. El próximo año, todos sus hijos, nietos y bisnietos celebran los **100 / 50** años de edad de doña Isabel.

B. Cosas de todos los días. Practice talking about your imaginary family, using the written cues. When you hear the corresponding number, form sentences using the words provided in the order given, making any necessary changes or additions. (Remember to repeat the correct answer.)

MODELO: (*you see*) 1. mi / familia / ser / muy / simpático   (*you hear*) uno →
(*you say*) *Mi* familia *es* muy *simpática*.

2. (nosotros) vivir / en / un / ciudad / pequeño
3. nuestro / casa / ser / bonito
4. mi / padres / siempre / leer / periódico / en / patio
5. (nosotros) siempre / comer / juntos (*together*)
6. este / noche / mi / hermanos / asistir / a / un / concierto
7. pero / yo / deber / estudiar / para / mi / clases

*This **Minidramas** videoclip is available on the DVD to accompany *Puntos de partida*, Eighth Edition.

Nombre _____ Fecha _____ Clase _____

CAPÍTULO **3**

VOCABULARIO Preparación

A. Hablando (*Speaking*) de la moda

Paso 1. Listen to the description of the clothing that a group of classmates wore to a popular night-club last Friday evening. As you listen, check the clothing worn by each person. (Check your answers in the Appendix.)

	ZAPATOS DE TENIS	CALCETINES	CAMISA	PANTALONES	CINTURÓN	CAMISETA	CORBATA
Ana							
Juan							
Luis							

Paso 2. Dictado. Now listen again. As you listen, write the colors mentioned for each article of cloth-ing. ¡OJO! The clothes are not listed in order. (Check your answers in the Appendix.)

ARTÍCULOS	COLOR(ES)
corbata	
camisa	
cinturón	
pantalones	
camiseta	
zapatos de tenis	
calcetines	

Capítulo 3 **45**

B. Identificaciones. Identify the items in the drawing after you hear the corresponding number. Begin each sentence with **Es un...** , **Es una...** , or **Son...**

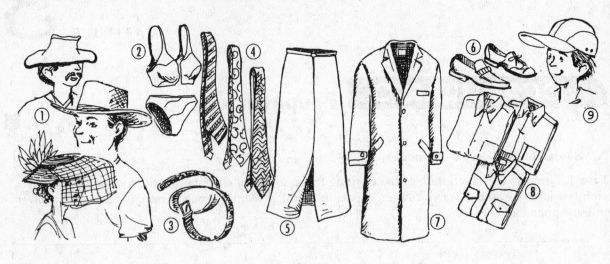

1. ...   2. ...   3. ...   4. ...   5. ...   6. ...   7. ...   8. ...   9. ...

C. Dictado: El inventario del Almacén Robles. Imagine that you and a coworker are doing a partial inventory for a department store. Listen to what your coworker says, and write the numbers in numerals next to the correct items. You will hear each number twice. **¡OJO!** The items are not listed in sequence. First, listen to the list of items. (Check your answers in the Appendix.)

ARTÍCULOS	NÚMERO (CANTIDAD)
pares de medias de nilón	
camisas blancas	
suéteres rojos	
pares de zapatos de tenis	
blusas azules	
faldas negras	

■■■Los hispanos hablan: ¿Qué importancia tiene la ropa para ti y tus amigos?

You will hear a student, Teresa, give an answer to the preceding question. After listening, pause and check all the statements that are true according to the passage. The following expressions appear in the passage.

una persona vale por lo que es	*a person's worth is determined by who he/she is*
aunque	*even though*
los harapos	*rags*

1. ☐ Teresa piensa que (*thinks that*) las modas son muy importantes.

2. ☐ Para ella, la persona es más importante que la ropa que usa.

3. ☐ La mayoría (*majority*) de sus amigos están de acuerdo con Teresa.

Now resume listening.

PRONUNCIACIÓN Y ORTOGRAFÍA — Stress and Written Accent Marks (Part 2)

A. Sílabas acentuadas. In Spanish, a written accent is required when a word does not follow the two basic rules.

1. The following words end in a vowel, **n**, or **s**. However, native speakers of Spanish do not pronounce these words according to the first basic rule. Repeat the following words, imitating the speaker.

   ac-**ción**   a-le-**mán**   sim-**pá**-ti-ca   be-**bé**
   fran-**cés**   es-**tás**   me-**nú**   te-**lé**-fo-no

2. These words break the second basic rule because they end in a consonant other than **n** or **s** and are not stressed on the last syllable. Repeat the following words, imitating the speaker.

   lá-piz   **ál**-bum   **Cá**-diz
   dó-lar   **Pé**-rez   **Gó**-mez

B. Más sílabas acentuadas. Here are other instances in which a Spanish word requires a written accent.

1. All words that are stressed on the third-to-last syllable must have a written accent mark on the stressed syllable, regardless of the final letter. Repeat the following words, imitating the speaker.

   bo-**lí**-gra-fo   ma-te-**má**-ti-cas   ar-**tí**-cu-lo
   ma-**trí**-cu-la   di-**fí**-ci-les   **Lá**-za-ro

2. When two consecutive vowels do not form a diphthong, the vowel that receives the spoken stress will have a written accent mark. This is very common in words ending in **-ía**. Compare the pronunciation of these pairs of words. Repeat each word, imitating the speaker.

   A-li-cia, po-li-cí-a
   Cle-men-cia, bio-lo-gí-a
   cien-cias, dí-a
   a-gua, grú-a (*construction crane*)

3. Some one-syllable words have accents to distinguish them from other words that sound like them. This accent is called a diacritical accent, and it has no effect on the pronunciation of the word. Repeat each word, imitating the speaker.

   él (*he*) / el (*the*)   tú (*you*) / tu (*your*)
   sí (*yes*) / si (*if*)   mí (*me*) / mi (*my*)

4. Interrogative and exclamatory words require a written accent on the stressed vowel. Repeat each sentence, imitating the speaker.

   ¿Qué estudias?   ¿Cómo te llamas?
   ¿Quién es tu profesora?   ¡Qué bueno! (*How great!*)
   ¿Dónde está Venezuela?

C. Palabras divididas. The following words have been divided into syllables for you. Read them when you hear the corresponding number. (Remember to repeat the correct answer.) ¡OJO! Some of the words will be unfamiliar to you. This should not be a problem because you have pronunciation rules to guide you.

1. nor-mal
2. prác-ti-co
3. á-ni-mo
4. a-na-to-mí-a
5. cu-le-bra
6. con-ver-ti-bles
7. ter-mó-me-tro
8. co-li-brí
9. con-di-cio-nal

D. Dictado. You will hear the following words. Each will be said twice. Listen carefully and write in a written accent where required. ¡OJO! Some of the words will be unfamiliar to you. This should not be a problem because you have the rules and the speaker's pronunciation to guide you. (Check your answers in the Appendix.)

1. metrica
2. distribuidor
3. anoche
4. Rosalia
5. actitud
6. sabiduria
7. jovenes
8. magico
9. esquema

GRAMÁTICA

9. Pointing Out People and Things • Demonstrative Adjectives (Part 2) and Pronouns

A. Gramática en acción: Suéteres a buenos precios. You will hear a dialogue in which Susana goes shopping for a sweater. After listening, pause and read each statement about the dialogue. Circle **C** (**cierto**) if the statement is true or **F** (**falso**) if it is false. If the information is not contained in or cannot be inferred from the dialogue, circle **ND** (**No lo dice** [*It doesn't say*]).

1. C F ND Susana busca un suéter de rayas.

2. C F ND Los suéteres de pura lana son más caros.

3. C F ND Los suéteres de pura lana cuestan 150 quetzales.

4. C F ND Los suéteres de rayas son de acrílico y cuestan 300 quetzales.

Vendedor (*salesperson*)   Susana   Jorge

Now resume listening.

B. ¿Cómo son estas cosas? Answer, using the oral cues and an appropriate form of the indicated demonstrative adjective. Remember to change the endings of the adjectives, and use **es** or **son,** as appropriate.

MODELO: (*you see*) ese / corbatas (*you hear*) verde → (*you say*) Esas corbatas son verdes.

1. ese / botas
2. este / pantalones
3. aquel / trajes
4. aquel / faldas
5. ese / vestidos

C. Recuerdos de su viaje a México. Your friends want to know all about your trip to Mexico. Answer their questions, using an appropriate form of the demonstrative adjective **aquel** and the oral cues.

MODELO: (*you hear and see*) ¿Qué tal el restaurante El Charro? (*you hear*) excelente →
(*you say*) ¡Aquel restaurante es excelente!

1. ¿Qué tal el Hotel Libertad?
2. ¿Y los dependientes del hotel?
3. ¿Qué tal la ropa del Mercado de la Merced?
4. ¿Y los parques de la capital?

10. Expressing Actions and States • *Tener, venir, preferir, querer,* and *poder;* Some Idioms with *tener*

A. Gramática en acción: Un mensaje telefónico: Dictado. You will hear the following answering machine message. It will be read twice. Listen carefully and write the missing words. (Check your answers in the Appendix.)

¡Hola, Jorge! Soy yo, Jaqui. Como tú sabes, yo siempre _____ comprar la ropa en los grandes almacenes. Pero hoy no _____ tiempo de ir al centro. _____ comprar una camisa para Juan Miguel, para su cumpleaños mañana. Creo que _____ encontrar algo en la boutique de este barrio. ¿_____ ayudarme? Juanmi es muy difícil de complacer en lo que _____ que ver con la moda... ¡Llámame! O mejor todavía... ¿por qué no _____ a mi casa? Un millón de gracias, Jorge. Hasta pronto.

B. Es la semana de exámenes. Practice telling about what you and your friends do during exam week, using the written and oral cues. ¡OJO! Remember that subject pronouns are not always used in Spanish.

MODELO: (*you hear*) nosotros (*you see*) tener muchos exámenes →
(*you say*) Tenemos muchos exámenes.

1. estar en la biblioteca
2. siempre venir conmigo (*with me*)
3. leer cien páginas
4. ¡ya no poder leer más!
5. querer regresar a la residencia
6. ...pero no poder

C. Situaciones y reacciones. You will hear a series of partial conversations. Each will be said twice. Listen carefully and circle the letter of the reaction or response that best completes each one.

1. a. Ay, ¡tú siempre tienes prisa!   b. Tienes razón, ¿verdad?
2. a. ¿Por qué tienes sueño?   b. Sí, tienes razón, pero tienes que estudiar más.
3. a. ¿Tienes que comer en un restaurante? b. ¿Tienes ganas de ir (*go*) a un restaurante?
4. a. ¿Cuántos años tienes?   b. La verdad es que tienes miedo, ¿no?
5. a. No, no tengo ganas de comprar ropa. b. ¿Cuántos años tiene la niña ahora?

11. Expressing Destination and Future Actions • *Ir; Ir + a + Infinitive;* The Contraction *al*

A. Gramática en acción: ¿Adónde vas? You will hear a dialogue in which Casandra asks her roommate Rosa where she is going. Then you will hear the following statements. Write the letter of the person who made each statement next to the statement.

a. Rosa   b. Casandra   c. Javier

1. _____ Voy a dar una fiesta este fin de semana.

2. _____ Voy al centro.

3. _____ Voy a comprar un vestido.

4. _____ Casandra y Rosa van a venir a mi fiesta.

B. ¿Adónde vas? You will hear a series of statements a friend might say about what you like to do or want to do. Using the words and phrases listed below, tell where you would go to do these activities. First, listen to the list.

| Almacén Robles | discoteca El Ciclón | Restaurante Gallego |
| biblioteca | mercado | universidad |

MODELO: (*you hear*) Te gusta estudiar y aprender cosas nuevas. →
(*you say*) Por eso voy a la universidad.

1. ...   2. ...   3. ...   4. ...   5. ...

C. Preguntas. You will hear a series of questions. Each will be said twice. Answer, using **ir + a +** infinitive and the written cues.

MODELO: (*you hear*) ¿Qué vas a comprar en la librería?   (*you see*) unos cuadernos →
(*you say*) Voy a comprar unos cuadernos.

1. tres horas   3. en McDonald's
2. a casa de un amigo   4. pantalones grises / un suéter rojo

D. ¿Qué va a hacer Gilberto este fin de semana?

Paso 1. You will hear a brief passage in which Gilberto tells what his plans are for this weekend. As you listen, number the following drawings so that they match the order in which Gilberto narrates his plans. Write the number in the smaller of the two blanks.

a. _____ _____

b. _____ _____

_____

_____

c. _____ _____

d. _____ _____

_____

_____

Paso 2. Now pause and, in the larger blanks, write a sentence that describes Gilberto's future actions. Use **ir** + **a** + *infinitive*. (Check your answers in the Appendix.)

Now resume listening.

UN POCO DE TODO (Para entregar)

A. Buscando regalos para papá. Listen to a conversation between a brother and sister, José and Ana, who are looking for gifts for their father. Do not be distracted by unfamiliar vocabulary. As you listen, circle only the items that they decide to buy.

B. *Listening Passage:* **El Rastro**

Antes de escuchar. Before you listen to the passage, pause and do the following prelistening exercise.

It is sometimes helpful to answer questions about yourself that are related to a passage that you will listen to or read. Answering the following questions will give you an idea of the information the passage might contain.

1. ¿Hay un mercado al aire libre en la ciudad donde tú vives?
2. Por lo general, ¿qué venden en los mercados al aire libre?
3. ¿Cómo crees que son los precios en un mercado al aire libre?
4. ¿Te gusta ir de compras?
5. ¿Te gusta regatear?
6. ¿Coleccionas algo? ¿Sellos (*Stamps*), monedas (*coins*), libros viejos, trenes (*trains*), muñecas (*dolls*)?

Now resume listening.

Listening Passage. Now, you will hear a passage about El Rastro, an open-air market in Madrid. The narrator is from Spain. The following words and phrases appear in the passage.

los sellos	*stamps*
las monedas	*coins*
los domingos	*on Sundays*
los puestos	*stalls*

Después de escuchar. Circle the letter of the phrase that best completes each sentence.

1. El Rastro es...
   a. una gran tienda.
   b. un centro comercial.
   c. un mercado con muchos puestos.
2. El Rastro está abierto (*open*)...
   a. todo el fin de semana.
   b. el domingo por la mañana.
   c. el domingo por la tarde.

3. En el Rastro venden...
   a. sólo ropa y zapatos.
   b. sólo cosas para coleccionistas (*collectors*).
   c. muchas cosas de todo tipo.
4. El Rastro está...
   a. en Madrid y es muy famoso.
   b. en España y es nuevo.
   c. en todas las ciudades de España.

Now resume listening.

C. Y para terminar… Entrevista. You will hear a series of questions. Each will be said twice. Answer based on your own experience. Pause and write the answers.

1. _____
2. _____
3. _____
4. _____
5. _____
6. _____
7. _____

VIDEOTECA   Minidramas*

Paso 1. José Miguel va de compras. In the following conversation, José Miguel is talking to an employee in a clothing store. José Miguel's lines will be read with pauses for repetition. But first, listen.

EMPLEADA: Buenos días. ¿En qué puedo servirle?

JOSÉ MIGUEL: ¿Qué precio tienen estas camisas?

EMPLEADA: Están en rebaja. Cuestan 40.000 sucres cada una.

JOSÉ MIGUEL: Es un precio excelente.

EMPLEADA: Sí. Las camisas son de puro algodón, y las tenemos de muchos colores. Aquí tiene una verde, otra roja, otra amarilla y otra azul. ¿Qué talla usa?

JOSÉ MIGUEL: La 38, por lo general.

EMPLEADA: Mire. Estos pantalones son perfectos para esta camisa. Con este pantalón negro y esta camisa azul, Ud. está a la última moda.

JOSÉ MIGUEL: Me gustan mucho los pantalones. Y la camisa también. ¿Me los puedo probar?

EMPLEADA: Sí, cómo no. Por allí están los probadores.

Paso 2. Aplicación. Now you will participate in a similar conversation, partially printed in your manual, in which you play the role of the customer. Complete the conversation using the written cues. (Remember to repeat the correct answer. If you wish, pause and write the correct answers.) Here are the cues for your conversation.

    zapatos de tenis   39   última moda

EMPLEADA: Buenas tardes. ¿En qué puedo servirle?

UD.: Busco un par de _____.

EMPLEADA: Pues, aquí tenemos de todo. ¿Qué número usa?

UD.: El _____, por lo general.

EMPLEADA: Tenemos varios estilos y colores…

UD.: Pues, quiero zapatos de _____.

EMPLEADA: Cómo no. Siéntese (*Sit down*) aquí, por favor. Le voy a traer (*I'm going to bring you*) varios estilos para probar.

_____

*This **Minidramas** videoclip is available on the DVD to accompany *Puntos de partida*, Eighth Edition.

PRUEBA CORTA

A. Cosas de todos los días. Practice talking about the price of different items of clothing, using the written cues. When you hear the corresponding number, form sentences using the words provided in the order given, making any necessary changes or additions. Note: **Cuesta** means *it costs*, **cuestan** means *they cost*.

> MODELO: (*you see*) 1. este / pantalones / negro / cuestan / $80   (*you hear*) uno →
> (*you say*) *Estos* pantalones *negros* cuestan *ochenta dólares.*

2. ese / chaqueta / azul / cuesta / $127
3. aquel / botas / pardo / cuestan / $215
4. este / vestido / amarillo / cuesta / $149
5. aquel / traje / gris / cuesta / $578
6. ese / ropa / cuesta / $1.069

B. ¿Qué van a llevar? You will hear a series of situations. Tell what each person might wear based on the information in each. First, listen to the possible items of clothing. ¡OJO! There is an extra item.

un abrigo de lana	un traje de baño
una camiseta de algodón	un traje y una corbata de seda
un cinturón	zapatos de tenis

> MODELO: (*you hear*) Los pantalones que llevo son muy grandes. →
> (*you say*) Voy a llevar un cinturón.

1. …   2. …   3. …   4. …   5. …

C. Apuntes (*Notes*): **De compras con Luis.** Luis has just received a bonus from his boss. He plans to spend all of it on clothes. Listen carefully to his narration and, as you listen, write the information requested. Write out all numbers. First, pause and read the requested information. (Check your answers in the Appendix.)

1. El dinero que tiene Luis: _____

2. El precio de la chaqueta: _____

3. El precio del reloj de oro (*gold*): _____

4. El material de los pantalones: _____

5. El material de las dos corbatas: _____

6. Lo que (*what*) no puede comprar: _____

7. El dinero que le queda (*remains*): _____

CAPÍTULO 4

VOCABULARIO Preparación

A. El horario (*schedule*) **de la profesora Velásquez**

Paso 1. Dictado. Imagine that you are Professor Velásquez's secretary and that you are filling in her weekly calendar. Listen carefully as she tells you her schedule for this week, and fill in the blanks in the calendar. Some of the entries have already been made. First, pause and look at the calendar. (Check your answers in the Appendix.)

lunes	martes	miércoles	jueves	viernes
mañana 10:45 AM : Clase de conversación	mañana _____ : dentista	mañana _____ :	mañana _____ :	mañana _____ :
tarde _____ :	tarde _____ :	tarde _____ :	tarde 3:00PM : Clase de español	tarde _____ :

Paso 2. Preguntas. Now you will hear a series of questions. Each will be said twice. Answer based on the information in **Paso 1.** Be sure to check your answers to **Paso 1** in the Appendix before beginning **Paso 2.** Follow the model.

> MODELO: (*you hear*) ¿Qué días enseña la profesora una clase de conversación? →
> (*you say*) El lunes y el viernes.

1. ... 2. ... 3. ... 4. ...

B. ¿Cuándo? Tell when your imaginary friends do the following things using the oral cues. Follow the model.

> MODELO: (*you see*) Anita estudia / la clase (*you hear*) antes de →
> (*you say*) Anita estudia antes de la clase.

1. Alicia escribe una carta / escucha la radio
2. Rosa trabaja / asistir a clases
3. Mis amigos bailan / las once de la noche
4. José lee / ir a la universidad

C. Identificación: ¿Qué hay en estos cuartos? Identify the following items when you hear the corresponding number. Begin each sentence with **Es un...** or **Es una...**

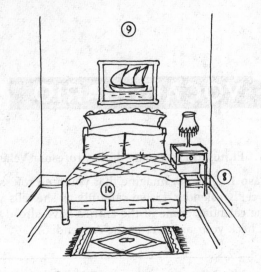

En la sala

1. ...   2. ...   3. ...   4. ...   5. ...   6. ...   7. ...

En la alcoba

8. ...   9. ...   10. ...

■■■Los hispanos hablan: Apuntes (*Notes*): ¿Qué cosas tienes en tu alcoba?

This question is answered by Xiomara. As you listen to the passage, jot down some of the things that she has in her room. The following words appear in the passage. (Check your answers in the Appendix.)

el abanico	*fan*
el tocador	*dressing table*
los cuadros	pinturas
la gata de peluche	*stuffed toy cat*
me regaló	*he gave me (as a gift)*

Lo que Xiomara tiene en su alcoba

_____

_____

_____

_____

_____

PRONUNCIACIÓN Y ORTOGRAFÍA *b* and *v*

Spanish **b** and **v** are pronounced exactly the same way. At the beginning of a phrase, or after **m** or **n**, **b** and **v** are pronounced like the English *b*, as a stop; that is, no air is allowed to escape through the lips. In all other positions, **b** and **v** are fricatives; that is, they are produced by allowing some air to escape through the lips. There is no equivalent for this sound in English.

A. Repeticiones. Repeat the following words and phrases, imitating the speaker. Note that the type of *b* sound you will hear is indicated at the beginning of the series.

1. [b]   bueno   viejo   barato   baño   hombre
2. [ƀ]   llevar   libro   pobre   abrigo   universidad
3. [b/ƀ] bueno / es bueno   busca / Ud. busca   bien / muy bien   en Venezuela / de Venezuela   visita / él visita
4. [b/ƀ] beber   bebida   vivir   biblioteca   vívido

B. Dictado. You will hear five sentences. Each will be said twice. Listen carefully and write what you hear. (Check your answers in the Appendix.)

1. _____
2. _____
3. _____
4. _____
5. _____

GRAMÁTICA

12. Expressing Actions • *Hacer, oír, poner, salir, traer, and ver*

A. Gramática en acción: Aspectos de la vida de Rigoberto. You will hear a series of statements about the following drawings. Listen carefully and write the number of each statement under the correct drawing.

a. _____   b. _____   c. _____   d. _____

B. Los jóvenes de hoy

Paso 1. Dictado. You will hear the following passage in which an adult complains about today's youth. It will be read twice. Listen carefully and fill in the missing words. (Check your answers in the Appendix.)

«¡Estos muchachos sólo quieren _____! No _____ sus

cosas en orden en sus cuartos... Los jóvenes de hoy día no

_____ nada bien; no son responsables... ¡Hasta quieren

_____ muchachas a sus cuartos!»

Paso 2. Preguntas. Now you will hear a series of questions that an adult might ask a young person. Each will be said twice. Answer based on your own experience. You will hear a possible answer. Pause and write your answers.

1. _____.

2. _____.

3. _____.

4. _____.

Now resume listening.

C. Encuesta. You will hear a series of statements. For each statement, check **siempre, a veces** (*sometimes*), or **nunca.** No answers will be given. The answers you choose should be true for you.

	SIEMPRE	A VECES	NUNCA		SIEMPRE	A VECES	NUNCA
1.	☐	☐	☐	4.	☐	☐	☐
2.	☐	☐	☐	5.	☐	☐	☐
3.	☐	☐	☐	6.	☐	☐	☐

D. Mis compañeros y yo. Form complete sentences about yourself and others, using the oral and written cues. The last two sentences will be negative.

> MODELO: (*you see*) Adela   (*you hear*) hacer ejercicio →
> (*you say*) Adela hace ejercicio.

1. yo   2. Tito y yo   3. tú   4. ellos   5. Marta

E. Soy buen compañero. Imagine that you want to impress your friend Sam, who is looking for a roommate. When you hear the corresponding number, form sentences that tell Sam what a good roommate you are. Make any necessary changes or additions. Repeat the correct sentence.

> MODELO: (*you see and hear*) uno   (*you see*) escuchar / noticias / por la mañana →
> (*you say*) Escucho las noticias por la mañana.

2. no hacer / mucho / fiestas
3. siempre / hacer / cama
4. no salir / tarde / sábados
5. no poner / televisor / doce / noche
6. siempre / poner / ropa / armario

13. Expressing Actions • Present Tense of Stem-Changing Verbs (Part 2)

A. Gramática en acción: ¿Una fiesta exitosa?

Paso 1. You will hear a series of statements about the following drawing. Circle **C** (**cierto**) if the statement is true or **F** (**falso**) if it is false. First pause and look at the drawing.

Now resume listening.

1. C F   2. C F   3. C F   4. C F   5. C F

Paso 2. Now pause and write the answers to the following questions. No answers will be given.

¿Es una fiesta exitosa? ¿Qué piensa usted? ¿Por qué?

_____

_____

_____

_____

_____

B. ¡Nunca más! You will hear a conversation between a husband and wife, Armando and Alicia, who are talking about a stationery store. It will be followed by a series of statements. Circle **C** (**cierto**) if the statement is true or **F** (**falso**) if it is false. In this exercise, you will practice listening for specific information.

1.   C F   En la papelería Franco piden precios muy caros.

2.   C F   A Armando no le gusta la papelería Franco.

3.   C F   Alicia dice (*says*) que va a volver a la papelería.

C. Encuesta. You will hear a series of statements about your habits. For each statement, check the appropriate response. No answers will be given. The answers you choose should be correct for you!

	SIEMPRE	CON FRECUENCIA	A VECES	¡NUNCA!
1.	☐	☐	☐	☐
2.	☐	☐	☐	☐
3.	☐	☐	☐	☐
4.	☐	☐	☐	☐
5.	☐	☐	☐	☐
6.	☐	☐	☐	☐

D. Un sábado típico en mi casa. Tell about the activities of your fictitious family on a typical Saturday. Use the written and oral cues.

1. yo
2. mis padres

3. mi hermana y yo
4. tú

E. Entrevista con los Sres. Ruiz. Interview Mr. and Mrs. Ruiz about some of the things they like to do. Use the written cues. You will hear an answer to each of your questions.

MODELO: (*you hear*) jugar al tenis →
(*you say*) ¿Juegan al tenis?   (*you hear*) No, no jugamos al tenis.

1. ...   2. ...   3. ...   4. ...

14. Expressing *-self/-selves* • Reflexive Pronouns (Part 1)

A. Gramática en acción: La rutina diaria de Andrés. You will hear a brief description of Andrés's daily routine. Then you will hear the following statements. Circle **C** (**cierto**) if the statement is true or **F** (**falso**) if it is false. If the information is not given in the description, circle **ND** (**No lo dice**).

1. C F ND   Andrés se levanta a las nueve de la mañana.

2. C F ND   Él se acuesta muy tarde.

3. C F ND   Se viste en el baño.

4. C F ND   Por lo general, Andrés tiene prisa por la mañana.

B. Encuesta. You will hear a series of statements about your habits. For each statement, check the appropriate response. No answers will be given. The answers you choose should be correct for you!

	SIEMPRE	CON FRECUENCIA	A VECES	¡NUNCA!
1.	☐	☐	☐	☐
2.	☐	☐	☐	☐
3.	☐	☐	☐	☐
4.	☐	☐	☐	☐
5.	☐	☐	☐	☐
6.	☐	☐	☐	☐

C. Hábitos y costumbres. Practice telling about some of the habits of the members of your fictitious family. Use the oral and written cues.

1. yo
2. mi primo y yo

3. mi hermanito
4. mis abuelos

D. ¿Qué van a hacer estas personas? When you hear the corresponding number, tell what the people in each drawing are going to do. ¡OJO! You will be using the **ir + a** + infinitive construction, and you will attach the reflexive pronouns to the infinitives. First, listen to the list of verbs.

acostarse   afeitarse   ducharse   quitarse   sentarse

1.

2.

3.

4.

5.

A. **¿Cuál es su casa?** You will hear a description of Raquel and Arturo's house, read by Raquel. Listen to the description and circle the number of the drawing that matches the description.

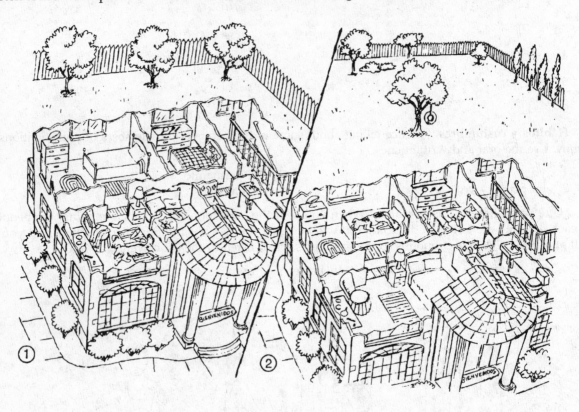

B. *Listening passage:* **Una casa hispana**

Antes de escuchar. Before you listen to the passage, pause and do the following prelistening exercises.

Paso 1. This passage will contain information about a house found in a Hispanic country. Check the specific information that you might expect to find in the passage.

☐ The speaker might talk about the different rooms in the house.

☐ The speaker might mention how many people are in his or her family.

☐ He or she might discuss the different architectural styles found in the Hispanic world.

Paso 2. Now complete the sentences with information that is true for your house or apartment. When a choice is given, circle the choice that is true for you.

1. Mi (casa/apartamento) tiene _____ alcoba(s) y _____ baño(s).

2. (Tiene / No tiene) sala.

3. (Tiene / No tiene) comedor.

4. Vivo allí con (mi familia / mis amigos/as). (Vivo sola/a [*alone*].)

5. Mi (casa/apartamento) (es / no es) típico/a de esta región o ciudad.

6. En la región donde vivo, (es necesario / no es necesario) tener calefacción (*heating*) en el invierno (*winter*).

7. Algo que (*Something that*) me gusta mucho de mi (casa/apartamento) es

_____.

8. Algo que no me gusta es _____.

Now resume listening.

Listening Passage. Now you will hear a passage about Alma's house. The following words appear in the passage.

afueras	*outskirts*
el vecindario	*neighborhood*
recámaras	*bedrooms*
juntos	*together*
árboles	*trees*
el clima	*climate*
calefacción	*heating*

Después de escuchar. Read the following true/false statements. Circle **C** (**cierto**) if the statement is true or **F** (**falso**) if it is false. If the information is not given in the passage, circle **ND** (**No lo dice**). Correct the statements that are false.

1. C F ND Todos los edificios en Panamá son de estilo colonial.

_____

2. C F ND Alma vive en el centro de la Ciudad de Panamá.

_____

3. C F ND Su casa es pequeña.

_____

4. C F ND Alma y su familia almuerzan en el comedor.

_____

5. C F ND La casa de Alma no tiene patio.

_____

Now resume listening.

C. Y para terminar... Entrevista. You will hear a series of questions. Each will be said twice. Answer based on your own experience. Pause and write the answers.

1. _____

2. _____

3. _____

4. _____

5. _____

6. _____

7. _____

8. _____

VIDEOTECA   Minidramas*

Paso 1. La rutina diaria. In this conversation, Diego and Antonio talk about their daily routine. Diego's lines will be read with pauses for repetition. But first, listen.

DIEGO: Dime, Antonio, ¿cómo es el horario de Uds.?

ANTONIO: Normalmente, yo me levanto a las siete y Juan se levanta a las seis y media. ¿A qué horas te levantas tú?

DIEGO: Si tengo clases, me levanto a las siete y media.

ANTONIO: ¡Perfecto! Primero Juan se baña y se afeita, después yo y por último tú.

DIEGO: ¿Y vuelven Uds. a casa para almorzar?

ANTONIO: Bueno, los lunes, miércoles y viernes sí vuelvo a casa para almorzar, porque no tengo clases por la tarde. Pero los martes y jueves almuerzo en la cafetería de la universidad. Juan no vuelve a casa para almorzar. Come en casa de su novia.

DIEGO: Muy bien. Entonces, los lunes, miércoles y viernes podemos almorzar aquí tú y yo. Antonio, creo que sí me va a gustar mucho vivir aquí.

Paso 2. Aplicación. Now you will participate in a similar conversation, partially printed in your manual, in which you play the role of Alfonso. Complete the conversation using the written cues. If you wish, pause and write the correct answers. Here are the cues for your conversation.

gracias   quién prepara la comida   el viernes por la tarde   especial

MARCOS: Bienvenido a nuestro apartamento, Alfonso.

ALFONSO: _____,[1] Marcos.

MARCOS: ¿Tienes alguna pregunta acerca del (*about the*) horario?

ALFONSO: Pues, sí. ¿_____[2] esta noche?

MARCOS: Bueno, Lucas prepara la comida esta noche, yo cocino (*cook*) el jueves y tú vas a cocinar el viernes.

ALFONSO: Perfecto. No tengo clases _____[3] y puedo preparar una

cena (*dinner*) _____.[4]

MARCOS: ¡Eso es magnífico!

---

*This **Minidramas** videoclip is available on the DVD to accompany *Puntos de partida*, Eighth Edition.

PRUEBA CORTA

A. Asociaciones. You will hear a series of statements. Circle the location with which you associate each statement.

1. a. la lámpara   b. el comedor   c. la cocina
2. a. la sala   b. el baño   c. la alcoba
3. a. el sofá   b. el armario   c. el lavabo
4. a. la piscina   b. el almacén   c. el garaje
5. a. la cocina   b. el comedor   c. la sala
6. a. la mesita   b. el plato   c. el sillón
7. a. la cómoda   b. el estante   c. el jardín

B. La rutina diaria. Practice talking about your daily routine, using the written cues. When you hear the corresponding number, form sentences using the words provided in the order given, making any necessary changes or additions.

MODELO: (*you see*) 1. (yo) despertarse y levantarse / 7:00 A.M.   (*you hear*) uno →
(*you say*) Me despierto y me levanto a las siete de la mañana.

2. (yo) ducharse / vestirse / y/ peinarse
3. hacer / el desayuno / y / sentarse a comer
4. hacer / la cama / y / salir / de casa / 8:00
5. después de las clases / ir / al gimnasio
6. hacer ejercicio / hasta / 3:30
7. volver a casa / y / poner el televisor
8. empezar / a preparar / comida
9. por fin / acostarse / 11:00 P.M. / y / dormirse

C. Apuntes. You will hear a brief paragraph that tells about a house for sale. Listen carefully and, while listening, write in the information requested. Write all numbers as numerals. First, listen to the new vocabulary and the requested information. (Check your answers in the Appendix.)

mide   *measures*
el metro   *meter*
por   *by (as in 3 meters by 2 meters)*
el vecindario   *neighborhood*

El número de alcobas: _____

El número de baños: _____

¿Cuántos metros mide la sala? _____

Esta casa está cerca de _____ y enfrente de _____.

La dirección (*address*) de la casa: _____

CAPÍTULO 5

VOCABULARIO Preparación

A. **¿Qué tiempo hace?** You will hear a series of weather conditions. Each will be said twice. Give the number of the drawing to which each corresponds, then repeat the description. First, pause and look at the drawings.

1.

2.

3.

4.

5.

6.

B. **¿Cuándo es… ?** Your Peruvian friend Evangelina wants to know when certain events take place, including a birth date (**una fecha de nacimiento**), an anniversary (**un aniversario**), and a national holiday (**una fiesta nacional**). Answer, using the written cues.

> MODELO: (*you hear*) ¿Cuándo es el cumpleaños de Nicolás? (*you see*) Sunday, May 4 →
> (*you say*) Es el domingo, cuatro de mayo.

1. Saturday, November 22
2. Wednesday, April 14
3. February 11, 1899
4. July 4, 1776

C. ¿Dónde está? You will hear a series of descriptions. Listen carefully and name the country, location, or item described. You will be listening for specific information about the location of the place or item. (Remember to repeat the correct answer.)

1. ...   2. ...   3. ...

4. ...   5. ...   6. ...

7. ...   8. ...   9. ...

■■■Los hispanos hablan: ¿De dónde eres?

You will hear three brief answers to this question. As you listen, write the information in the spaces provided. First, pause and look at the information for which you need to listen. (Check your answers in the Appendix.)

Habla José.

Ciudad: _____ País: _____

El clima: _____

La gente (*people*): _____

¿Hay una universidad en la ciudad?   Sí   No

Habla Clara.

Ciudad: _____ País: _____

El clima: _____

La gente: _____

¿Hay una universidad en la ciudad?   Sí   No

Habla Diana.

Ciudad: _____ País: _____

El clima: _____

La gente: _____

¿Hay una universidad en la ciudad?   Sí   No

PRONUNCIACIÓN Y ORTOGRAFÍA *r* and *rr*

The letter **r** has two pronunciations in Spanish: the trilled **r** (written as **rr** between vowels or as **r** at the beginning of a word), and the flap **r,** which appears in all other positions. Because mispronunciations can alter the meaning of a word, it is important to distinguish between these two pronunciations of the Spanish **r.** For example: **coro** (*chorus*) and **corro** (*I run*).

The flap **r** is similar to the sound produced by the rapid pronunciation of *tt* and *dd* in the English words *Betty* and *ladder*.

A. Repeticiones. Listen to these word pairs. Then repeat them.

> *Petty* / pero
>
> *sadder* / Sara
>
> *motor* / moro

B. Más repeticiones. Repeat the following words, phrases, and sentences, imitating the speaker.

1.	arte	gracias	para	vender	triste
2.	ruso	Roberto	real	reportero	rebelde
3.	burro	corral	carro	barra	corro

4. el extranjero
   el precio del cuaderno
   el nombre correcto
   Enrique, Carlos y Rosita
   las residencias
   una mujer refinada
   Puerto Rico
   El perro está en el corral.
   Soy el primo de Roberto Ramírez.
   Estos errores son raros.

C. ¿R o rr? You will hear a series of words. Each will be said twice. Circle the letter of the word you hear.

1. a. ahora   b. ahorra
2. a. caro   b. carro
3. a. coro   b. corro
4. a. coral   b. corral
5. a. pero   b. perro

GRAMÁTICA

15. ¿Qué están haciendo? • Present Progressive: *Estar* + *-ndo*

A. Gramática en acción: ¿Qué está haciendo Elisa? Dictado. You will hear a passage that describes the activities of Elisa on her day off. Listen carefully and write the missing words. (Check your answers in the Appendix.)

Elisa es periodista. Por eso escribe mucho y habla mucho por teléfono en su trabajo. Pero ahora

no _____ _____. ¿Qué _____ _____? _____ _____ en casa. _____ _____ música, _____ una novela

y _____ un café.

B. ¿Qué están haciendo? You will hear a series of sentences. Each will be said twice. Write the number of each statement next to the item that corresponds to the activity mentioned. First, listen to the list of items.

a. _____ el restaurante

b. _____ las bicicletas y la pelota (*ball*)

c. _____ el libro

d. _____ la computadora

e. _____ la música

C. Descripción: ¿Qué están haciendo en este momento? Using the present progressive of the following verbs, tell what each person in the Hernández family is doing at the moment. For the exercise, don't attach the reflexive pronouns to the present participle. First, listen to the list of verbs.

afeitarse   bañarse   dormir   jugar   ponerse   vestirse

MODELO: (*you hear*) uno → (*you say*) El bebé está durmiendo.

2. …   3. …   4. …   5. …   6. …

D. ¡Sé lo que (*I know what*) **estás haciendo!** Your friend Amalia will say where she is and you will guess what she might be doing there. You will hear each of her statements twice. You will hear a possible answer. First, listen to the list of possible actions.

estudiar   preparar el almuerzo

leer   trabajar

mirar la tele

MODELO: (*you hear*) Estoy en mi alcoba. → (*you say*) Estás estudiando, ¿verdad?

1. …   2. …   3. …   4. …

16. ¿*Ser* o *estar*? • Summary of the Uses of *ser* and *estar*

A. Gramática en acción: Una conversación de larga distancia. You will hear one side of a telephone conversation between a husband and his wife who is on a business trip. Then you will hear a series of questions from the dialogue. Circle the letter of the best response to each.

1. a. Estoy en Nueva York.   b. Estoy cansada, pero estoy bien.
2. a. Es el Sr. Miró.   b. Es muy moderno.
3. a. Estoy trabajando.   b. Hace buen tiempo.
4. a. Hace buen tiempo.   b. Son las once y media.

B. ¿Qué pregunta hiciste? (*What question did you ask?*) You will hear a series of statements that contain **ser** or **estar.** Each will be said twice. Circle the letter of the question that corresponds to each.

1. a. ¿Cómo estás?   b. ¿Cómo eres?
2. a. ¿Cómo están?   b. ¿Cómo son?
3. a. ¿Dónde estás?   b. ¿De dónde eres?
4. a. ¿Dónde está el consejero?   b. ¿De dónde es el consejero?
5. a. ¿De quién es la blusa?   b. ¿De qué es la blusa?

C. Marcos, ¿qué tal? When you hear the corresponding number, tell how your friend Marcos seems to be feeling on these different occasions. Use one of the following adjectives. Use Marcos's name only in the first sentence. First, listen to the list of adjectives.

        contento   furioso   nervioso   preocupado   triste

1.   2.   3.

4.   5.

1. ...   2. ...   3. ...   4. ...   5. ...

D. ¿Quiénes son? Imagine that the people in this photograph are your relatives. Tell who they are and describe them, using the oral cues and the appropriate forms of **ser** or **estar.** All the cues are about the couple on the right. Begin your first answer with **Son...**

1. ...   2. ...   3. ...   4. ...   5. ...   6. ...

17. Describing • Comparisons

A. Gramática en acción: México D.F. y Sevilla, España

Paso 1. La comparación. Listen to a comparison between Mexico City (**el Distrito Federal [D.F.]**) and Sevilla.

Paso 2. ¿Qué recuerda Ud.? Pause and complete the following sentences based on the comparison. (Check your answers in the Appendix.)

1. Sevilla es _____ bonita _____ la Ciudad de México.

2. Sevilla tiene _____ edificios altos _____ el D.F.

3. En el D.F. no hace _____ calor _____ en Sevilla.

4. Sevilla no tiene _____ habitantes _____ el D.F.

Now resume listening.

B. La rutina de Alicia. The following chart shows Alicia's routine for weekdays and weekends. You will hear a series of statements about the chart. Each will be said twice. Circle **C** if the statement is true or **F** if it is false, according to the chart. First pause and read the chart.

ACCIÓN	DE LUNES A VIERNES	SÁBADO Y DOMINGO
levantarse	6:30	9:30
bañarse	7:15	10:00
trabajar	8 horas	1 hora
almorzar	20 minutos	30 minutos
divertirse	1 hora	8 horas
acostarse	11:00	11:00

1. C F   2. C F   3. C F   4. C F   5. C F

C. Un desacuerdo. Imagine that you and your friend Lourdes don't agree on anything! React to her statements negatively, following the model and using the cues.

> MODELO: (*you hear and see*) Los amigos son más importantes que la familia.
> (*you hear*) tan → (*you say*) No, los amigos son tan importantes como la familia.

1. El invierno es más bonito que el verano.
2. Hace tanto calor en Florida como en Alaska.
3. La clase de cálculo es menos difícil que la clase de física.
4. Los niños juegan más videojuegos (*videogames*) que los adultos.

UN POCO DE TODO | (Para entregar)

A. En la plaza Santa Ana

Paso 1. ¿Qué pasa? You will hear a series of statements about the following drawing. Each will be said twice. Circle **C** if the statement is true or **F** if it is false. First, pause and look at the drawing.

1. C F   2. C F   3. C F   4. C F   5. C F

Paso 2. Descripción. Now pause and write five sentences that describe the drawing. You can talk about the weather, what the people are doing, how they seem to be feeling, their clothing, and so on. You can also make comparisons.

1. _____
2. _____
3. _____
4. _____
5. _____

Now resume listening.

B. *Listening Passage:* Hablando del clima

Antes de escuchar. Before you listen to the passage, pause and do the following prelistening exercises.

Paso 1. Read the following true/false statements. As you read them, try to infer the information the passage will give you, as well as the specific information for which you need to listen.

1. En las regiones tropicales, por lo general, hay una estación seca (*dry*) y una lluviosa (*rainy*).

2. En Latinoamérica, no hace frío en ninguna (*any*) región.

3. Hay climas muy variados en el mundo hispánico.

4. En Sudamérica, las estaciones del año son opuestas a las (*opposite to those*) de los países del Hemisferio Norte.

Paso 2. You probably do know quite a bit about the climate in most of Latin America. That information will be fairly easy for you to recognize in the listening passage. Read the next set of true/false statements, and try to infer what type of information you need to listen for regarding the person who will narrate the passage.

La persona que habla...

1. es de Vermont.
2. prefiere el frío del invierno.

3. no sabe (*doesn't know how to*) esquiar.
4. quiere vivir en los Andes.

A la persona que habla...

5. no le gustan las estaciones lluviosas en los países tropicales.

Now resume listening.

Listening Passage. Now, you will hear a passage about the climate in different regions of the Hispanic world. This passage is read by Nicanor, a friend of Susana's. The following words appear in the passage.

seca	*dry*
lluviosa	*rainy*
yo lo tengo claro	*it's clear to me*

Después de escuchar. Here is another version of the true/false statements you did in **Antes de escuchar.** Circle **C** if the statement is true or **F** if it is false. Then correct the statements that are false, according to the passage.

1. C F Nicanor es de Vermont.

   _____

2. C F A Nicanor no le gusta el frío.

   _____

3. C F En el mundo hispánico, hay climas muy variados.

   _____

4. C F En Sudamérica no hace frío en ninguna región.

   _____

5. C F A Nicanor le gustaría (*would like*) vivir en los Andes.

   _____

6. C F Cuando es verano en el Hemisferio Norte, también es verano en el Hemisferio Sur.

   _____

Now resume listening.

C. Y para terminar... Entrevista. You will hear a series of questions. Each will be said twice. Answer based on your own experience. Write out all numbers. Pause and write the answers.

1. _____
2. _____
3. _____
4. _____
5. _____
6. _____

VIDEOTECA Minidramas*

Paso 1. Hablando por teléfono. In this conversation, Carolina Díaz calls her friend Marta Durán Benítez. Marta's father, Manolo Durán, takes a phone message for his daughter. Carolina's lines will be read with pauses for repetition. But first, listen.

MANOLO: ¿Diga?

CAROLINA: Buenos días. Habla Carolina Díaz. ¿Está Marta?

MANOLO: No, Carolina. Marta no está en este momento. Está en el parque con su tío abuelo. ¿Quieres dejarle un recado?

CAROLINA: Sí, muchas gracias. Me gustaría decirle que si quiere venir esta tarde a jugar conmigo. Hace buen tiempo y podríamos ir a jugar afuera.

MANOLO: Muy bien, Carolina. Yo le doy el recado. Saluda a tus padres de mi parte, por favor.

CAROLINA: Sí. Adiós.

MANOLO: Adiós.

Paso 2. Aplicación. Now you will participate in a similar conversation, partially printed in your manual, in which you play the role of Susanita. Complete the conversation using the written cues. Here are the cues for your conversation. ¡OJO! The cues are not in order.

Habla Susanita Márquez.	Adiós.
Hola.	No, gracias.
¿Está Elena?	Puedo llamar más tarde.
Muchas gracias.	

EDUARDO: ¿Bueno? (*Hello?*)

SUSANITA: _____.¹ ¿_____?²

EDUARDO: ¿De parte de quién, por favor? (*Who's calling, please?*)

SUSANITA: _____³

EDUARDO: Hola, Susanita. Lo siento, pero Elena está en casa de su tía. ¿Quieres dejar un recado?

SUSANITA: _____,⁴ _____⁵

EDUARDO: Está bien. Elena va a regresar dentro de (*within*) una hora.

SUSANITA: _____,⁶ _____⁷

EDUARDO: Adiós.

---

*This **Minidramas** videoclip is available on the DVD to accompany *Puntos de partida*, Eighth Edition.

PRUEBA CORTA

A. Comparaciones. You will hear a series of statements about the following chart. Each will be said twice. Circle **C** if the statement is true, or **F** if it is false. First, pause and read the chart.

PAÍS	POBLACIÓN (HABITANTES)	ÁREA (MILLAS CUADRADAS) (*SQUARE MILES*)	TEMPERATURA COSTAL / TEMPERATURA INTERIOR EN GRADOS *FAHRENHEIT*	NÚMERO DE USUARIOS DEL INTERNET
Costa Rica	4.133.884	19.730	90° / 63°	1.000.000
Guatemala	12.728.111	42.042	82° / 68°	756.000
Nicaragua	5.675.356	50.838	77° / 79°	140.000
México	108.700.891	756.066	120° / 61°	18.622.000

Now resume listening.

1. C F   2. C F   3. C F   4. C F   5. C F   6. C F

B. La nueva profesora costa rricense. Tell about the new professor, using the written cues. When you hear the corresponding number, form sentences using the words provided in the order given, making any necessary changes or additions. You will be given a choice of verbs. Choose the correct one.

> MODELO: (*you see*) 1. la profesora / (ser / estar) / Isabel Darío
> (*you hear*) uno → (*you say*) La profesora es Isabel Darío.

2. la profesora / (ser / estar) / de La Cruz, Costa Rica
3. La Cruz / (ser / estar) / lejos de la capital
4. la profesora / (ser / estar) / cansada por el viaje
5. ella / se (ser / estar) / quedando con unos amigos
6. la profesora / (ser / estar) / inteligente y simpática
7. los estudiantes / (ser / estar) / contentos con la nueva profesora

C. Hablando de viajes. Imagine that you will travel to a variety of places this year. Answer the questions you hear about each of your trips using the written cues. ¡OJO! The questions may vary slightly from those in the model. Change your answers accordingly.

> MODELO: (*you see*) 3/30 / fresco
> (*you hear*) ¿Cuándo sales para Detroit? → (*you say*) Salgo el treinta de marzo.
> (*you hear*) ¿Y qué tiempo hace allí? → (*you say*) Hace fresco.

1. 7/15 / calor
2. 12/1 / nevando
3. 1/10 / sol
4. 5/24 / viento

CAPÍTULO **6**

VOCABULARIO Preparación

A. Definiciones. You will hear a series of definitions. Each will be said twice. Circle the letter of the word defined by each.

1. a. la zanahoria   b. los huevos
2. a. la lechuga   b. la langosta
3. a. la leche   b. el vino blanco
4. a. un postre   b. un sándwich
5. a. el almuerzo   b. la cena
6. a. los espárragos   b. el agua mineral

B. Identificaciones. Identify the following foods when you hear the corresponding number. Use the definite article in your answer.

1.   2.   3.   4.

5.   6.   7.   8.

C. Categorías. You will hear a series of words. Repeat each word, telling in what category it belongs: **un tipo de carne, un marisco, una fruta, una verdura, un postre,** or **una bebida.**

MODELO: (you hear) el té → (you say) El té es una bebida.

1. …   2. …   3. …   4. …   5. …

D. ¿Qué sabe y a quién conoce?

Paso 1. Mis amigos. You will hear a brief paragraph about some of the things your friends know and whom they know. Listen and write either **sí** or **no** under the corresponding item. Two items have been done for you. (Check your answers in the Appendix before you begin **Paso 2**.)

NOMBRE	BAILAR	A JUAN	JUGAR AL TENIS	A MIS PADRES	ESTA CIUDAD
Enrique	sí	no			
Roberto					
Susana					

Paso 2. ¿Qué recuerda Ud.? Now pause and complete the following statements with information from the completed chart. (Check your answers in the Appendix.)

1. Roberto y Susana _____ jugar al tenis.

2. Susana _____ bailar.

3. Nadie (*No one*) _____ a Juan.

4. Roberto y Enrique _____ bien la ciudad.

Now resume listening.

■■■Los hispanos hablan: ¿Qué no te gusta nada comer?

You will hear answers to this question from Clara, Xiomara, and Teresa. As they describe the foods that they do not like, check the appropriate boxes. Go back and listen again, if necessary. First, listen to the list of foods. (Check your answers in the Appendix.)

	CLARA	XIOMARA	TERESA
1. huevos	☐	☐	☐
2. verduras	☐	☐	☐
3. oreja de cerdo (*pig's ear*)	☐	☐	☐
4. mondongo (*tripe soup*)	☐	☐	☐
5. hamburguesas con pepinillos (*pickles*)	☐	☐	☐
6. caracoles (*snails*)	☐	☐	☐
7. comida rápida	☐	☐	☐
8. mantequilla	☐	☐	☐
9. platos sofisticados	☐	☐	☐

PRONUNCIACIÓN Y ORTOGRAFÍA *d*

A. Repeticiones. Spanish **d** has two pronunciations. At the beginning of a phrase or sentence and after **n** or **l,** it is pronounced similarly to English *d* as in *dog:* [d], that is, as a stop. Listen to these words and repeat them after the speaker.

[d]   diez   ¿dónde?   venden   condición   falda   el doctor

In all other cases, **d** is pronounced like the English sound *th* in *another* but softer: [đ], that is, as a fricative. Listen and repeat the following words.

[đ]   adiós   seda   ciudad   usted   cuadros   la doctora

B. Entonación. Repeat the following sentences, imitating the speaker. Pay close attention to the intonation.

¿Dónde está el dinero?   ¿Qué estudia Ud.?

Dos y diez son doce.   Venden de todo, ¿verdad?

C. A escoger. You will hear a series of words containing the letter **d.** Each will be said twice. Circle the letter of the **d** sound you hear.

1. a. [d]   b. [đ]   4. a. [d]   b. [đ]
2. a. [d]   b. [đ]   5. a. [d]   b. [đ]
3. a. [d]   b. [đ]

GRAMÁTICA

18. Expressing *what* or *who(m)* • Direct Objects (Part 2): The Personal *a*; Direct Object Pronouns

A. Gramática en acción: De compras en el supermercado: Encuesta. You will hear the names of various foods. Each will be said twice. Write in the blank the name of the food mentioned, then check the appropriate answer. No answers will be given. The answers you choose should be correct for you! (Check the answers for the food names in the Appendix.)

1. _____

☐ Siempre las como.

☐ Las como a veces.

☐ Nunca las como.

2. _____

☐ Siempre lo como.

☐ Lo como a veces.

☐ Nunca lo como.

3. _____

☐ Siempre la tomo.

☐ La tomo a veces.

☐ Nunca la tomo.

4. _____

☐ Siempre los como.

☐ Los como a veces.

☐ Nunca los como.

B. En la cocina. Imagine that you are preparing a meal, and your friend Pablo is in the kitchen helping you. Answer his questions, using object pronouns and the written cues. You will hear each question twice.

> MODELO: (*you hear*) ¿Necesitas la olla (*pot*) ahora?
> (*you see*) sí → (*you say*) ¿La olla? Sí, la necesito.
> (*you see*) no → (*you say*) ¿La olla? No, no la necesito todavía.

1. no
2. sí
3. sí
4. no

C. Entre amigos... Imagine that your friend Manuel, who hasn't seen you for a while, wants to know when you can get together again. Answer his questions, using the written cues. You will hear each question twice.

1. esta noche
2. para mañana
3. 4:00
4. café La Rioja

D. Hablando de los estudios. You will hear a series of questions a parent or friend might ask about things you have already done. Each will be said twice. Answer, using **acabo de** and a direct object pronoun. Attach the direct object pronoun to the infinitive when you answer.

MODELO: (*you hear*) ¿Por qué no escribes la composición? → (*you say*) Acabo de escribirla.

1. ...   2. ...   3. ...   4. ...

19. Expressing Negation • Indefinite and Negative Words

A. Gramática en acción: ¿Un refrigerador típico?

Paso 1. You will hear a series of questions about the following drawing. Circle the letter of the best answer to each, based on the drawing.

1. a. No, no hay nada.   b. Sí, hay algo.
2. a. Sí, hay fruta y pan.   b. No, no hay fruta y tampoco hay pan.
3. a. No, no hay ninguna manzana.   b. Sí, hay manzanas.
4. a. No, nadie compra comida.   b. Sí, alguien compra comida.

Paso 2. Now pause and write what you usually have and don't have in your refrigerator. No answers will be given.

En mi refrigerador siempre hay _____

_____

Nunca hay _____

_____

Now resume listening.

B. En la cocina de Diego y Antonio. You will hear a dialogue between roommates Diego and Antonio. Diego has just returned home; and he is hungry. Then you will hear a series of statements. Circle **C** if the statement is true or **F** if it is false. If the information is not contained in the dialogue, circle **ND (No lo dice)**.

1. C F ND

2. C F ND

3. C F ND

4. C F ND

C. Descripción. You will hear a series of questions. Answer, according to the drawings.

MODELO: (*you hear*) ¿Hay algo en la pizarra? →
(*you say*) Sí, hay algo en la pizarra. Hay unas palabras.

1.

2.

hablo hablamos
hablas habláis
habla hablan

3.

4.

5.

D. ¡Por eso no come nadie allí! You will hear a series of questions about a very unpopular restaurant. Each will be said twice. Answer, using the double negative.

    MODELO: (*you hear*) ¿Sirven algunos postres especiales? →
                  (*you say*) No, no sirven ningún postre especial.

    1. ...   2. ...   3. ...   4. ....

20. Influencing Others • Commands (Part 1): Formal Commands

A. Gramática en acción: Una receta para guacamole

Paso 1. You will hear the following recipe for guacamole. It contains several formal commands. Read the recipe silently, along with the speakers.

El guacamole

Ingredientes:
1 aguacate[a]
1 diente de ajo,[b] prensado[c]
1 tomate
jugo de un limón
sal
un poco de cilantro fresco[d]

Cómo se prepara
Corte el aguacate y el tomate en trozos[e] pequeños. Añada el jugo del limón, el ajo, el cilantro y la sal a su gustó. Mezcle bien todos los ingredientes y sírvalo con tortillas de maíz[f] fritas.

[a]*avocado* [b]*diente... clove of garlic* [c]*crushed* [d]*fresh* [e]*pieces* [f]*corn*

Paso 2. Now pause and write the command forms of the following infinitive verbs in the spaces. (Check your answers in the Appendix.)

    1. servir: _____
    2. añadir (*to add*): _____
    3. mezclar (*to mix*): _____
    4. cortar: _____

B. ¿Qué acaban de decir? You will hear a series of commands. Write the number of the command you hear next to the corresponding drawing. You will hear each statement twice. ¡OJO! There is an extra drawing.

    a. _____   b. _____   c. _____

    d. _____   e. _____

C. Profesora por un día... Imagine that you are the Spanish professor for the day. Practice telling your students what they should do, using the oral cues. Use **Uds.** commands.

    1. ...   2. ...   3. ...   4. ...   5. ...

D. La dieta del Sr. Casiano. Mr. Casiano is on a diet and you are his doctor. He will ask you whether or not he can eat certain things. Answer his questions, using affirmative or negative commands and direct object pronouns.

    MODELO: (*you hear*) ¿Puedo comer chocolate? (*you see*) No,... →
                       (*you say*) No, no lo coma.

    1. No,...   2. No,...   3. No,...   4. Sí,...   5. Sí,...

E. Un nuevo restaurante

Paso 1. You will hear an ad for a new restaurant that is opening soon. Listen carefully and check the appropriate boxes based on the information you hear in the ad. First, listen to the list of actions. (Check your answers in the Appendix.)

	SÍ	NO
hacer reservaciones	☐	☐
vestirse formalmente	☐	☐
pedir el pescado	☐	☐
pedir una hamburguesa	☐	☐
llegar temprano	☐	☐
pagar con tarjeta de crédito	☐	☐
pagar al contado (*in cash*)	☐	☐

Paso 2. Now pause and read the following recommendations. Check the recommendations that you would give a friend who wants to visit this restaurant. (Remember to check your answers to **Paso 1** in the Appendix before beginning **Paso 2.**)

    1. ☐ No recomiendo que hagas reservaciones antes de ir a El Caribe.

    2. ☐ Recomiendo que llegues temprano.

    3. ☐ Recomiendo que vayas a El Caribe si te gusta mucho la carne.

    4. ☐ Recomiendo que te vistas con ropa informal.

    5. ☐ No recomiendo que lleves a toda tu familia.

    6. ☐ Recomiendo que pagues con tarjeta de crédito o al contado.

Now resume listening.

UN POCO DE TODO | (Para entregar)

A. ¿Qué va a pedir Juan? Juan and his friend Marta are in a restaurant. Listen to their conversation and circle the items that Juan is going to order. In this exercise, you will practice listening for specific information. First, pause and look at the drawing.

B. *Listening passage:* **La vida social en los bares de España**

Antes de escuchar. Before you listen to the passage, pause and do the following prelistening exercises.

Many aspects of social life and nightlife in Spain are different from those of the United States. Check the ones that you think apply *only* to Spain.

☐ Hay muchos bares. ¡A veces hay dos en cada calle (*street*)!

☐ La familia entera, padres e hijos pequeños, va al bar.

☐ Por lo general, no se sirve comida.

☐ Es costumbre pedir tapas: pequeños platos de comidas diversas.

Now resume listening.

Listening Passage. Now you will hear a passage about the many types of bars that are part of Spanish social life. The following words and phrases appear in the passage.

no tienen nada que ver con	*they have nothing to do with*
casero	*homemade, home-style*
sevillanos	personas de Sevilla
el ambiente	*atmosphere*

Después de escuchar. Go back and listen to the passage again. Then pause, and complete the following sentences with words chosen from the list.

amigos   bar   café   frío   Madrid   tapas   tarde   Sevilla

1. En España, los españoles van con frecuencia a un _____ o a un _____

   para pasar el tiempo con los _____ y los compañeros.

2. En los bares, sirven _____, que son pequeños platos de comidas diversas.

3. Julia dice que prefiere la ciudad de _____ para divertirse. Allí no hace

   _____ en el invierno y la gente puede salir muy _____ todo el año.

Now resume listening.

C. Y para terminar... Entrevista. You will hear a series of questions. Each will be said twice. Answer based on your own experience. Use direct object pronouns in your answers, if possible. Pause and write the answers.

1. _____
2. _____
3. _____
4. _____
5. _____
6. _____
7. _____

VIDEOTECA   Minidramas*

Paso 1. En el restaurante. In this conversation, Manolo Durán and his wife, Lola Benítez, have dinner in a restaurant. Manolo's lines will be read with pauses for repetition. But first, listen.

CAMARERO: ¿Ya saben lo que desean de comer los señores?

MANOLO: Creo que sí, pero, ¿qué recomienda Ud.?

CAMARERO: Hoy tenemos un plato especial: gambas al limón con arroz, un plato ligero y delicioso. Y también tenemos un salmón buenísimo que acaba de llegar esta tarde.

LOLA: ¡Qué rico! Yo quiero las gambas, por favor.

MANOLO: Eh, para mí, el bistec estilo argentino, poco asado. Y una ensalada mixta para dos.

CAMARERO: ¿Y para empezar? Tenemos una sopa de ajo (*garlic*) muy rica.

LOLA: Para mí, una sopa, por favor.

MANOLO: Y para mí también. Y le dice al chef que por favor le ponga un poco de atún a la ensalada.

CAMARERO: Muy bien, señor.

Paso 2. Aplicación. Now you will participate in a similar conversation, partially printed in your manual, in which you play the role of the **cliente** in a restaurant. Complete the conversation using the written cues. Here are the cues for your conversation. ¡OJO! The cues are not in order.

el flan de naranja   un coctel de camarones

los tacos de pollo   un vino blanco

CAMARERA: ¿Sabe ya lo que desea de comer?

CLIENTE: Sí. Favor de traerme _____.[1]

CAMARERA: Sí, cómo no. ¿Y para empezar? Tenemos una gran variedad de antojitos (*appetizers*) que seguramente le van a gustar.

CLIENTE: Bueno, tráigame _____,[2] por favor.

---

*This **Minidramas** videoclip is available on the DVD to accompany *Puntos de partida*, Eighth Edition.

CAMARERA: ¿Algo de postre?

CLIENTE: Sí, quiero _____,³ por favor.

CAMARERA: Muy bien. ¿Y para beber?

CLIENTE: ¿Me puede traer _____?⁴

CAMARERA: Sí. Se lo traigo en seguida (*I'll bring it to you right away*).

PRUEBA CORTA

A. Los hispanos hablan: ¿Qué te gusta mucho comer?

In this passage, Clara tells about two dishes typical of Spain: **el cocido** and **el gazpacho.** Then you will hear a series of statements. Circle **C** if the statement is true or **F** if it is false. The following words appear in the passage.

el hueso de codillo	*leg bone (as in ham)*
la morcilla	*blood sausage*
el pepino	*cucumber*
el pimiento	*pepper*
el ajo	*garlic*
el aceite de oliva	*olive oil*
el vinagre	*vinegar*
echarle por encima	*to sprinkle on top of it*
trocitos	*little bits (pieces)*

1. C F   2. C F   3. C F   4. C F

B. Cosas de todos los días. Practice talking about a new restaurant, using the written cues. When you hear the corresponding number, form sentences using the words provided in the order given, making any necessary changes or additions. When you are given a choice between verbs or words, choose the correct one.

MODELO: (*you see*) 1. ¿(saber / conocer) / tú / un buen restaurante?
(*you hear*) uno → (*you say*) ¿Conoces un buen restaurante?

2. sí, yo / (saber / conocer) / un buen restaurante
3. ellos / (la / lo) / acabar de / abrir
4. yo / (saber / conocer) / al dueño (*owner*)
5. ellos / preparar / unos camarones deliciosos
6. ellos / (las / los) / cocinar / en vino blanco
7. no hay / (algo / nada) / malo en el menú
8. yo / (siempre / nunca) / cenar allí

C. ¡Qué maleducados! Mr. Alarcón's children have not been behaving lately, and he is constantly telling them what to do and what not to do. Play the role of Mr. Alarcón, using the oral cues.

MODELO: (*you hear*) no jugar en la sala → (*you say*) No jueguen en la sala.

1. ...   2. ...   3. ...   4. ...   5. ...

CAPÍTULO 7

VOCABULARIO Preparación

A. Definiciones. You will hear a series of definitions. Each will be said twice. Circle the letter of the word that is defined by each. ¡OJO! There may be more than one answer in some cases.

1. a. el avión   b. la playa   c. el océano
2. a. el billete   b. la estación de trenes   c. el aeropuerto
3. a. el hotel   b. el restaurante   c. la llegada
4. a. el puerto   b. el mar   c. las montañas

B. Identificaciones. Identify the items after you hear the corresponding number. Begin each sentence with **Es un...** , **Es una...** , or **Son...**

1. ...   2. ...   3. ...   4. ...   5. ...

C. Hablando de viajes... Using the oral and written cues, tell your friend Benito, who has never traveled by plane, the steps he should follow to make an airplane trip.

> MODELO: (*you see*) Primero... (*you hear*) llamar a la agencia de viajes →
> (*you say*) Primero llamas a la agencia de viajes.

1. pedir...
2. El día del viaje,...
3. pasar por...
4. Después...
5. Cuando anuncian la salida del vuelo,...
6. Por fin...

■■■Los hispanos hablan: Unas vacaciones inolvidables (*unforgettable*)

You will hear Cecilia's description of an unforgettable vacation. Then you will hear a series of statements. Circle **C** if the statement is true or **F** if it is false. The following words appear in the description.

hace un año	*one year ago*	hacernos cargo de	*take care of*
veranear	pasar el verano	la aduana	*customs*
partimos	*we left*	las valijas	las maletas
el colectivo	*type of taxi shared by several passengers*	armamos la carpa	*we set up the tent*

1. C F Cecilia y su amiga pasaron (*spent*) el verano en las montañas.

2. C F Los padres de las muchachas pagaron (*paid for*) el viaje.

3. C F Cecilia y su amiga pasaron un mes en el Uruguay.

4. C F Había (*There were*) otra gente joven en la playa donde se quedaron Cecilia y su amiga.

PRONUNCIACIÓN Y ORTOGRAFÍA *g, gu,* and *j*

A. Repeticiones. In Spanish, the letter **g** followed by **e** or **i** has the same sound as the letter **j** followed by any vowel. This sound [x] is similar to the English *h*. The pronunciation of this sound varies, depending on the region or country of origin of the speaker. Note the difference in the pronunciation of these words.

España:	Jorge	jueves	general	álgebra
el Caribe:	Jorge	jueves	general	álgebra

Repeat the following words, imitating the speaker.

1. [x] general   gigante   geranio   2. [x] jamón   Juan   pasaje

Now, say the following words when you hear the corresponding number. Repeat the correct pronunciation after the speaker.

3. gimnasio 4. giralda 5. rojo 6. jipijapa

B. El sonido [g]. When the letter **g** is followed by the vowels **a, o,** or **u** or by the combination **ue** or **ui**, its pronunciation is very similar to the letter *g* in the English word *get:* [g]. It is also pronounced this way at the beginning of a word, after a pause, or after the letter **n.**

Repeat the following words, imitating the speaker.

[g] ángulo gusto gato Miguel guitarra

Now, say the following words when you hear the corresponding number. Repeat the correct pronunciation after the speaker.

1. gorila 2. grande 3. guerrilla 4. Guevara

C. El sonido [g]. In all other positions, the Spanish **g** is a fricative [g̶]. It has a softer sound produced by allowing some air to escape when it is pronounced. There is no exact equivalent for this variant in English.

Repeat the following words, imitating the speaker.

1. [g] abrigo algodón el gato el gusto los gorilas
2. [g] / [g̶] un grupo el grupo gracias las gracias un gato el gato
3. [x] / [g̶] gigante jugos juguete

Now, read the following sentences when you hear the corresponding numbers. Repeat the correct pronunciation after the speaker.

4. ¡Qué ganga!
5. Domingo es guapo y delgado.
6. Tengo algunas amigas guatemaltecas.
7. La guitarra de Guillermo es de Gijón.

D. Dictado. You will hear four sentences. Each will be said twice. Listen carefully and write what you hear. (Check your answers in the Appendix.)

1. _____
2. _____
3. _____
4. _____

GRAMÁTICA

21. Expressing *to who(m)* or *for who(m)* • Indirect Object Pronouns; *Dar* and *decir*

A. Gramática en acción: En el aeropuerto. You will hear two brief conversations. Write the number of each next to the correct location. (Check your answers in the Appendix.)

———— En el mostrador

———— En el control de la seguridad

B. Las vacaciones de primavera. You will hear a brief passage about what Javier told his parents. Then you will hear a series of incomplete statements. Circle the letter of the phrase that best completes each statement.

1. a. nunca les pide dinero.
   b. les pide mucho dinero para sus clases.
2. a. pedirles dinero para este semestre.
   b. pedirles dinero para el pasaje de avión.
3. a. Javier les pide mucho dinero.
   b. Javier es trabajador.
4. a. dinero para el boleto y comida.
   b. un cheque para sus clases.

C. Encuesta. You will hear a series of statements. Indicate what is true for you by checking the appropriate answer. No answers will be given. The answers you choose should be correct for you!

	SIEMPRE	A VECES	¡NUNCA!			SIEMPRE	A VECES	¡NUNCA!
1.	☐	☐	☐		5.	☐	☐	☐
2.	☐	☐	☐		6.	☐	☐	☐
3.	☐	☐	☐		7.	☐	☐	☐
4.	☐	☐	☐		8.	☐	☐	☐

D. En casa, durante la cena. Practice telling for whom the following things are being done, according to the model.

MODELO: (*you see*) Mi padre sirve el guacamole. (*you hear*) a nosotros →
(*you say*) Mi padre *nos* sirve el guacamole.

1. Mi madre sirve la sopa.
2. Ahora ella prepara la ensalada.
3. Mi hermano trae el café.
4. Rosalinda da postre.

E. Descripción. When you hear the corresponding number, tell what the following people are doing, using the written cues with indirect object pronouns.

EN LA FIESTA DE ANIVERSARIO DE LOS SRES. MORENO

1. Susana: regalar   2. Miguel: mandar   3. Tito: regalar

EN CASA, DURANTE EL DESAYUNO

4. Pedro: dar
5. Marta: dar
6. Luis: servir / todos

22. Expressing Likes and Dislikes • *Gustar* (Part 2)

A. Gramática en acción: Los chilenos viajeros. You will hear a series of statements about the following ad. Circle **C** if the statement is true or **F** if it is false. If the information is not contained in or cannot be inferred from the description, circle **ND** (**No lo dice**). First pause and read the ad. Do not be distracted by unfamiliar vocabulary.

Now resume listening.

1. C F ND   2. C F ND   3. C F ND   4. C F ND

B. Los gustos de nuestra familia. You will hear the father of the following family make some statements about the family's likes and dislikes. Circle **C** if a statement is true or **F** if it is false, based on the drawing. First, pause and look at the drawing.

1. C F   2. C F   3. C F   4. C F   5. C F

C. ¡Vamos de vacaciones! Pero... ¿adónde? You and your family can't decide where to go on vacation. You will hear what each person likes. Then decide where each person would like to go, using a location from the following list. There may be more than one answer in some cases. First, listen to the list. You will hear a possible answer.

Disneylandia	las playas de México
la Florida	quedarse en casa
Nueva York	Roma

MODELO: (*you hear*) A mi padre le gusta mucho jugar al golf. →
(*you say*) Le gustaría ir a la Florida.

1. ...   2. ...   3. ...   4. ...   5. ...

D. ¿Qué le gusta? ¿Qué no le gusta? Using the written cues, tell what you like or dislike about the following situations or locations. You will hear a possible answer.

MODELO: (*you see and hear*) ¿En la universidad? (*you see*) fiestas / exámenes →
(*you say*) Me gustan las fiestas. No me gustan los exámenes.

1. ¿En la playa?   jugar al voleibol / sol
2. ¿En un restaurante?   comida / música
3. ¿En un parque?   flores / insectos
4. ¿En la cafetería?   hablar con mis amigos / comida

23. Talking About the Past (Part 1) • Preterite of Regular Verbs and of *dar, hacer, ir,* and *ser*

A. Gramática en acción: Un viaje a la República Dominicana. Elisa is a reporter who recently traveled to the Dominican Republic to write an article. You will hear Elisa tell about her trip. The passage is narrated in the past.

Now pause and read the following statements. Circle **C** if the statement is true or **F** if it is false. Correct the false statements. (Check your answers in the Appendix.)

1. C F Elisa viajó a la República Dominicana en barco.

   _____

2. C F El viaje a la República Dominicana fue corto.

   _____

3. C F Elisa visitó muchos lugares interesantes de la isla.

   _____

4. C F Elisa habló con muchas personas en la República Dominicana.

   _____

5. C F A Elisa no le gustó su viaje.

   _____

Now resume listening.

B. **¿Qué hizo Nadia anoche?** You will hear a series of statements. Each will be said twice. Write the number of each statement next to the drawing that is described by that statement. First, pause and look at the drawings. Nadia's friend is Guadalupe.

a. _____

b. _____

c. _____

d. _____

e. _____

f. _____

g. _____

h. _____

i. _____

C. ¿Qué pasó ayer? Practice telling what the following people did yesterday, using the oral and written cues. Do not say the subject pronouns in parentheses.

ANTES DE LA FIESTA

1. (yo)
2. mi compañero
3. (nosotros)

ANTES DEL EXAMEN DE QUÍMICA

4. Nati y yo
5. (tú)
6. todos

D. ¿Quién hizo... ? You will hear a series of questions about what you and your friends did last night (**anoche**). Answer according to the drawings. First, pause and look at the drawings.

MODELO: (*you hear*) ¿Quién habló por teléfono? → (*you say*) Alicia habló por teléfono.

1. ... 2. ... 3. ... 4. ...

UN POCO DE TODO | (Para entregar)

A. En el periódico: Anuncios. You will hear an ad for a Mexican airline company. Then you will hear a series of statements. Circle **C** if the statement is true or **F** if it is false, based on the information contained in the ad and the following chart of departures. First, listen to the following phrases you will hear in this activity.

un viaje de negocios   *a business trip*   un viaje de placer   *a trip for pleasure*

MIAMI 10 vuelos semanales

SALIDAS	LUNES	MARTES	MIERCOLES	JUEVES	VIERNES	SABADO	DOMINGO
	11:50 Y 15.05	16:10	11 50 Y 16 10	15.15	11 50 Y 11 05	15 15	15.05

1. C F   2. C F   3. C F   4. C F

B. *Listening Passage:* Un anuncio turístico

Antes de escuchar. Pause and do the following prelistening exercises.

Paso 1. Find out how much you know about Mexico's tourist attractions by answering the following questions. As you read the questions, try to infer the information the passage will give you, as well as the specific information for which you need to listen.

1. ¿Conoce Ud. México? ¿Sabe que la Ciudad de México es una de las ciudades más grandes del mundo, más grande aun (*even*) que Nueva York? ¡Tiene más de 25.000.000 de habitantes!
2. ¿Sabe Ud. el nombre de algunos de los pueblos indígenas (*native*) de México? Los olmecas y los toltecas son menos famosos que otros. ¿Cuáles son los más famosos?

Paso 2. Empareje (*Match*) el nombre de la ciudad mexicana con la atracción turística por la cual (*by which*) se conoce.

1. _____ la Ciudad de México
2. _____ Teotihuacán
3. _____ Acapulco
4. _____ Taxco
5. _____ Cancún

a. ruinas mayas y playas bonitas
b. objetos de plata (*silver*) y artesanías (*crafts*)
c. las Pirámides del Sol y de la Luna (*Moon*)
d. playas
e. el mejor museo antropológico del mundo

Now resume listening.

Listening Passage. Now, you will hear a travel ad about an excursion to Mexico. The following words appear in the passage.

mezclar	*to mix*	el submarinismo	*snorkeling*
la plata	*silver*	saborear	*to taste*
relajarse	*to relax*	tentadora	*tempting*
broncearse	*to get a tan*	las plazas	*spaces (on the tour)*

Después de escuchar. Indicate the things that the tourists can do on this trip.

1. ☐ Pueden broncearse.

2. ☐ Hacen submarinismo.

3. ☐ Escalan (*They climb*) unas montañas muy altas.

4. ☐ Compran objetos de plata.

5. ☐ Pueden nadar en dos playas, por lo menos (*at least*).

6. ☐ Ven las ruinas de Machu Picchu.

7. ☐ Visitan un museo antropológico.

Now resume listening.

C. Y para terminar… Entrevista. You will hear a series of questions. Each will be said twice. Answer based on your own experience. Pause and write the answers.

1. _____

2. _____

3. _____

4. _____

5. _____

6. _____

VIDEOTECA   Minidramas*

Paso 1. En la agencia de viajes. In this conversation, you will hear Elisa Velasco making arrangements for a trip to the Galápagos Islands. Listen and read along with the speakers.

SR. GÓMEZ: ¿Cuánto tiempo piensa quedarse en las islas?

ELISA: Me gustaría pasar una semana allí. Quiero viajar en avión desde Quito. ¿Cuánto cuesta un boleto de ida y vuelta?

SR. GÓMEZ: Cuesta 615.000 sucres si Ud. viaja el sábado en la mañana.

ELISA: Está bien.

SR. GÓMEZ: ¿Desea que le haga una reservación de hotel también?

ELISA: Sí, por favor.

SR. GÓMEZ: Entonces, le hago las siguientes reservaciones: el avión sale de Quito a las islas el sábado 13 y seis noches de reservación en el hotel de la isla Santa Cruz.

ELISA: Perfecto. Muchas gracias.

SR. GÓMEZ: No hay por qué. ¿Cómo le gustaría pagar? ¿Lo de siempre?

ELISA: Sí, con tarjeta de crédito… ¡la del periódico, por supuesto!

---

*This **Minidramas** videoclip is available on the DVD to accompany *Puntos de partida*, Eighth Edition.

Paso 2. Aplicación. Now you will participate in a similar conversation, partially printed in your manual, in which you play the role of a client who wishes to purchase train tickets. Complete the conversation using the written cues. Here are the cues for your conversation. ¡OJO! The cues are not in order.

> gracias / aquí / tenerlos
> darme (*command*) / billete de ida y vuelta
> a qué hora / salir / tren / para Colón

CLIENTE: ¿_____?[1]

AGENTE: A las ocho y media de la mañana.

CLIENTE: _____,[2] por favor.

AGENTE: Son veinte balboas (*monetary unit of Panama*).

CLIENTE: _____.[3]

PRUEBA CORTA

A. Cosas de todos los días: De vacaciones. Practice talking about your and your family's recent trip, using the written cues. When you hear the corresponding number, form sentences using the words provided in the order given, making any necessary changes or additions.

> MODELO: (*you see*) 1. mi familia y yo / ir de vacaciones   (*you hear*) uno →
> (*you say*) Mi familia y yo *fuimos* de vacaciones.

2. el agente / recomendarnos / viaje a Cancún
3. (nosotros) viajar / Cancún / en avión
4. avión / no / hacer escalas
5. (nosotros) llegar / a / hotel / sin problemas
6. el recepcionista / darnos / cuarto con balcón (*balcony*)
7. mi / hermanos / nadar / la piscina (*swimming pool*)
8. (yo) tomar / el sol
9. nuestra madre / sacar / fotografías
10. nuestro padre / mandarles / tarjetas postales / a los amigos
11. gustarnos / mucho / viaje

B. Apuntes. You will hear a conversation between a tourist who is interested in traveling to Cancún and a travel agent. Listen carefully and write down the requested information. First, listen to the list of information that is being requested. (Check your answers in the Appendix.)

el tipo de boleto que el turista quiere: _____

la fecha de salida: _____

la fecha de regreso (*return*): _____

la sección y la clase en que va a viajar: _____

la ciudad de la cual (*from which*) va a salir el avión: _____

el tipo de hotel que quiere: _____

el nombre del hotel en que se va a quedar: _____

CAPÍTULO

8

VOCABULARIO Preparación

A. ¿Una fiesta familiar típica? You will hear a description of Sara's last family gathering. Then you will hear a series of statements. Circle **C** if the statement is true or **F** if it is false. If the information is not given, circle **ND** (**No lo dice**).

1. C F ND Según lo que dice Sara, las fiestas familiares normalmente son muy divertidas.

2. C F ND A la tía Eustacia le gusta discutir (*argue*) con el padre de Sara.

3. C F ND Normalmente, los primos de Sara se portan mal (*behave poorly*) en las fiestas familiares.

4. C F ND Sara no lo pasa bien nunca en las fiestas familiares.

5. C F ND Los hermanos de Sara discuten mucho con sus padres.

B. Asociaciones. With which of the following celebrations do you associate the descriptions that you hear? Each will be said twice. ¡OJO! There might be more than one possible answer in some cases.

1. a. La Navidad
   b. el Día de la Raza
   c. el cumpleaños
2. a. el Día de San Valentín
   b. la Pascua
   c. el Cuatro de Julio
3. a. el Día de los Reyes Magos
   b. el Día de Acción de Gracias
   c. el Día de los Muertos
4. a. la quinceañera
   b. el Día de los Reyes Magos
   c. el día del santo

C. ¿Cómo reacciona Ud.? Practice telling how you react to these situations, using the oral and written cues. Use the word **cuando** in each sentence.

MODELO: (*you see*) Me olvido del cumpleaños de mi madre. (*you hear*) ponerme triste →
(*you say*) Me pongo triste cuando me olvido del cumpleaños de mi madre.

1. Mis padres me quitan (*take away*) el coche.
2. Veo una película triste.
3. Saco buenas notas (*grades*).
4. Tengo que hacer cola.

■■■Los hispanos hablan: Una fiesta inolvidable (*unforgettable*)

You will hear Karen and Xiomara talk about two unforgettable parties. The following words appear in the descriptions.

las damas	*ladies (maids of honor)*	orgulloso	*proud*
el vals	*waltz*	el brindis	*toast*
duró	*lasted*	he pasado	*I have spent*
estuvo presente	*were there*		

Now, pause and indicate the statements that can be inferred from the information in the two descriptions.

1. ☐ La quinceañera (fiesta de los quince años) es una fiesta importante para Karen y Xiomara.

2. ☐ Hay muchos invitados en estas fiestas.

3. ☐ La quinceañera es una fiesta que dura (*lasts*) hasta muy tarde.

4. ☐ Karen y Xiomara celebraron su quinceañera en los Estados Unidos.

5. ☐ En estas fiestas hay música.

Now resume listening.

PRONUNCIACIÓN Y ORTOGRAFÍA — *c* and *qu*

A. El sonido [k]. The [k] sound in Spanish can be written two ways: before the vowels **a, o,** and **u** it is written as **c**; before **i** and **e**, it is written as **qu**. The letter **k** itself appears only in words that are borrowed from other languages. Unlike the English [k] sound, the Spanish sound is not aspirated; that is, no air is allowed to escape when it is pronounced. Compare the following pairs of English words in which the first [k] sound is aspirated and the second is not.

can / scan   cold / scold   kit / skit

B. Repeticiones. Repeat the following words, imitating the speaker. Remember to pronounce the [k] sound without aspiration.

1. casa	cosa	rico	loca	roca
2. ¿quién?	Quito	aquí	¿qué?	pequeño
3. kilo	kilogramo	kerosén	kilómetro	karate

Now, when you hear the corresponding number, read the following words. Repeat the correct pronunciation after the speaker.

4. paquete   6. química   8. camarones
5. quinceañera   7. comida   9. ¿por qué?

C. Dictado. You will hear a series of words. Each will be said twice. Listen carefully and write what you hear. ¡OJO! Some of the words may be unfamiliar to you. Concentrate on the sounds. (Check your answers in the Appendix.)

1. _____   4. _____

2. _____   5. _____

3. _____   6. _____

Nombre _____ Fecha _____ Clase _____

GRAMÁTICA

24. Talking About the Past (Part 2) • Irregular Preterites

A. Gramática en acción: La fiesta de la Noche Vieja

Paso 1. You will hear a series of statements about the following drawing. Circle **C** if the statement is true or **F** if it is false.

1. C F
2. C F
3. C F

4. C F
5. C F
6. C F

Paso 2. Now pause and circle the letter of the correct verb to indicate what each person did based on the drawing.

1. Marina _____ hablando por teléfono.   a. pudo   b. estuvo

2. Javier y Gema le _____ un regalo a Paco.   a. trajeron   b. quisieron

3. Sultán _____ mucho ruido.   a. dio   b. hizo

4. Ernesto _____ su copa de champán en el televisior.   a. puso   b. pudo

Now resume listening.

B. Encuesta: Hablando de lo que pasó ayer. You will hear a series of statements about what happened to you yesterday. For each statement, check the appropriate answer. No answers will be given. The answers you choose should be correct for you!

1. ☐ Sí   ☐ No

2. ☐ Sí   ☐ No

3. ☐ Sí   ☐ No

4. ☐ Sí   ☐ No

5. ☐ Sí   ☐ No

6. ☐ Sí   ☐ No

7. ☐ Sí   ☐ No

8. ☐ Sí   ☐ No

C. Una fiesta de cumpleaños. Tell what happened at the party, using the written and oral cues.

MODELO: (*you see*) estar en casa de Mario   (*you hear*) todos →
(*you say*) Todos estuvimos en casa de Mario.

1. tener que preparar la comida
2. venir con regalos
3. hacer mucho ruido
4. ¡estar estupenda!

D. Preguntas: ¿Qué pasó durante su fiesta de cumpleaños? You will hear a series of questions. Each will be said twice. Answer, using the written cues. Use object pronouns when possible.

1. en mi casa
2. sí: venir todos mis tíos y primos
3. a su novia
4. sobre una mesa
5. mi primo

25. Talking About the Past (Part 3) • Preterite of Stem-Changing Verbs

A. Gramática en acción: La quinceañera de Lupe Carrasco: Dictado. You will hear a series of sentences about the following drawing. Listen carefully and write the missing words. (Check your answers in the Appendix.)

1. Lupe _____ con un vestido blanco muy elegante.

2. Mientras cortaba el pastel de cumpleaños, Lupe _____ mucho.

3. También _____ para todas las fotos que sacaron.

4. Lupe _____ un deseo al cortar el pastel.

5. Ella _____ guardar el deseo en secreto.

6. En la fiesta _____ refrescos.

7. Todos _____ mucho en la fiesta.

8. Los invitados _____ a la una y media de la mañana.

B. La fiesta de sorpresa

Paso 1. You will hear a brief paragraph, narrated by Ernesto, about a surprise party. Listen carefully and check the appropriate actions for each person. First, pause and look at the chart. (Check your answers in the Appendix.)

PERSONA	VESTIRSE ELEGANTEMENTE	SENTIRSE MAL	DORMIR TODA LA TARDE	PREFERIR QUEDARSE EN CASA
Julia				
Verónica				
Tomás				
Ernesto (el narrador)				

Paso 2. You will hear a series of statements about the preceding paragraph. Each will be said twice. Circle **C** if the statement is true or **F** if it is false. If the information is not given, circle **ND** (**No lo dice**).

1. C F ND

2. C F ND

3. C F ND

4. C F ND

5. C F ND

C. ¿Qué le pasó a Antonio?

Tell what happened to Antonio when you hear the corresponding number. First, listen to the beginning of Antonio's story.

Raquel Morales invitó a Antonio a una fiesta en su casa. Antonio le dijo a Raquel que él asistiría (*would attend*), pero todo le salió mal. En primer lugar...

1. no recordar llevar refrescos
2. perder la dirección de la Srta. Morales
3. llegar muy tarde a la fiesta
4. no divertirse
5. sentirse enfermo después de la fiesta
6. acostarse muy tarde
7. dormir mal esa noche
8. despertarse a las cinco de la mañana
9. tener que ir a clases de todas formas (*anyway*)

26. Expressing Direct and Indirect Objects Together • Double Object Pronouns

A. Gramática en acción: Berta habla de la fiesta de Anita

Paso 1. You will hear a series of statements. Write the number of each statement under the corresponding drawing.

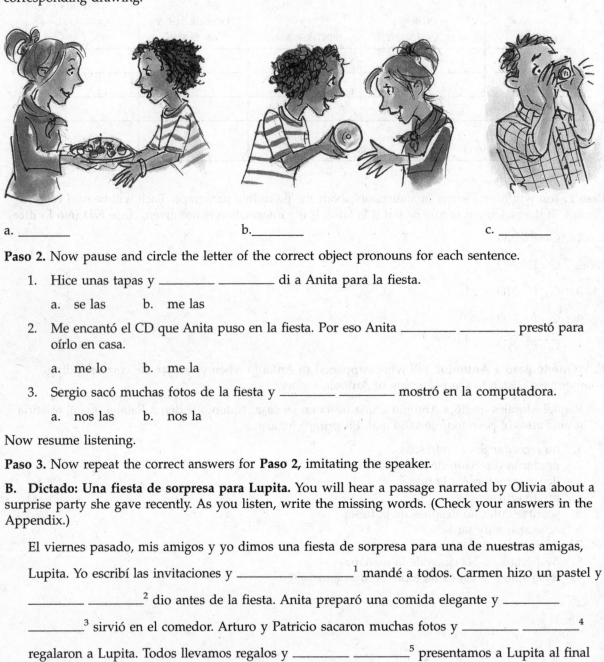

a. _____   b. _____   c. _____

Paso 2. Now pause and circle the letter of the correct object pronouns for each sentence.

1. Hice unas tapas y _____ _____ di a Anita para la fiesta.

   a. se las   b. me las

2. Me encantó el CD que Anita puso en la fiesta. Por eso Anita _____ _____ prestó para oírlo en casa.

   a. me lo   b. me la

3. Sergio sacó muchas fotos de la fiesta y _____ _____ mostró en la computadora.

   a. nos las   b. nos la

Now resume listening.

Paso 3. Now repeat the correct answers for **Paso 2,** imitating the speaker.

B. Dictado: Una fiesta de sorpresa para Lupita. You will hear a passage narrated by Olivia about a surprise party she gave recently. As you listen, write the missing words. (Check your answers in the Appendix.)

El viernes pasado, mis amigos y yo dimos una fiesta de sorpresa para una de nuestras amigas,

Lupita. Yo escribí las invitaciones y _____ _____[1] mandé a todos. Carmen hizo un pastel y

_____ _____[2] dio antes de la fiesta. Anita preparó una comida elegante y _____

_____[3] sirvió en el comedor. Arturo y Patricio sacaron muchas fotos y _____ _____[4]

regalaron a Lupita. Todos llevamos regalos y _____ _____[5] presentamos a Lupita al final

de la fiesta. ¡Lupita nos dijo que fue una fiesta maravillosa!

C. En casa, durante la cena. During dinner, your brother asks about the different foods that might be left. He will say each question twice. Listen carefully and circle the items to which he is referring.

> MODELO: (*you hear*) ¿Hay más? ¿Me la pasas, por favor?
> (*you see*) la sopa   el pan   el pescado →
>
> (*you circle*) (la sopa)

1. las galletas   la fruta   el helado
2. la carne   el postre   los camarones
3. la leche   el vino   las arvejas
4. las papas fritas   la cerveza   el pastel

D. ¿Dónde está? Carolina would like to borrow some things from you. Tell her to whom you gave each item, basing your answer on the written cues and selecting the correct pronouns. You will hear each of Carolina's questions twice.

> MODELO: (*you hear*) Oye, ¿dónde está tu diccionario?
> (*you see*) Se (lo/la) presté a Nicolás. Él (lo/la) necesita para un examen. →
> (*you say*) Se lo presté a Nicolás. Él lo necesita para un examen.

1. Se (lo/la) presté a Nicolás. Él (lo/la) necesita para un viaje.
2. Se (los/las) presté a Teresa. Ella (los/las) necesita para su fiesta.
3. Se (la/las) presté a Juan. Él (la/las) necesita para escribir un trabajo.
4. Se (lo/la) presté a Nina. Ella (lo/la) necesita para ir al parque.

UN POCO DE TODO (Para entregar)

A. Un día típico. You will hear a description of a day in Ángela's life, narrated in the past. Then you will hear a series of statements. Circle **C** if the statement is true or **F** if it is false. If the information is not given, circle **ND** (**No lo dice**).

1. C F ND   Ángela se acostó tarde ayer.

2. C F ND   Ángela se levantó a las seis y media.

3. C F ND   Ángela se puso furiosa cuando llegó a la oficina.

4. C F ND   El jefe (*boss*) le dio mucho trabajo.

5. C F ND   Los padres de Ángela viven lejos de ella.

6. C F ND   Cuando Ángela se acostó, se durmió inmediatamente.

B. *Listening Passage:* El carnaval

Antes de escuchar. You will hear a passage about carnival celebrations. The following words appear in the passage.

pagana	*pagan, not religious*
la Cuaresma	*Lent*
las máscaras	*masks*
los disfraces	*costumes*
caricaturescos	*cartoonish, satirical*
se mezclan	*are blended*
inolvidable	*unforgettable*

Listening Passage. Here is the passage. First, listen to it to get a general idea of the content. Then go back and listen again for specific information.

Después de escuchar. Indicate the statements that contain information that you *cannot* infer from the listening passage.

1. ☐ El carnaval es una tradición exclusivamente europea.

2. ☐ A pesar de (*In spite of*) las diferencias, las celebraciones de carnaval tienen muchas semejanzas (*similarities*).

3. ☐ El carnaval celebra la llegada del buen tiempo.

4. ☐ Los mejores carnavales se celebran en Europa.

5. ☐ La gran diferencia entre el carnaval de Río y los otros carnavales es que el de Río se celebra en un mes distinto (diferente).

6. ☐ La persona que habla tuvo gran dificultad con el idioma en Río de Janeiro.

7. ☐ La persona que habla quiere ir al *Mardi Gras* de Nueva Orleáns el próximo año.

Now resume listening.

C. Y para terminar… Entrevista. You will hear a series of questions. Each will be said twice. Answer based on your own experience. Pause and write the answers.

1. _____

2. _____

3. _____

4. _____

5. _____

6. _____

7. _____

VIDEOTECA   Minidramas*

Paso 1. La despedida. In the following conversation, Manolo Durán and his family are saying good-bye to other family members after a celebration. Listen and read along with the speakers.

JAIME: Bueno, hasta otro, hermano.
MANOLO: ¡Y que sea pronto!
ELENA: Hasta luego. Nos divertimos mucho, ¿eh?
ANA: Que tengáis buen viaje.
PEDRO: Nos mandaréis copias de las fotos, ¿no?
JAIME: Por supuesto que sí. Ha sido maravilloso veros. ¡Que haya suerte!

---

*This **Minidramas** videoclip is available on the DVD to accompany *Puntos de partida*, Eighth Edition.

Paso 2. Aplicación. In the preceding conversation, Manolo and his family were saying good-bye. It is also important to greet your guests. You will hear a series of conversations. Listen carefully and indicate when each conversation might take place: at the beginning of a party, during the party, or at the end of the party.

1. a. a la llegada   b. durante la fiesta   c. a la despedida
2. a. a la llegada   b. durante la fiesta   c. a la despedida
3. a. a la llegada   b. durante la fiesta   c. a la despedida
4. a. a la llegada   b. durante la fiesta   c. a la despedida

PRUEBA CORTA

A. Preparativos para la fiesta de Gilberto. The speaker will ask you several questions about Gilberto's birthday party. You will hear each question twice. Circle the letter of the best answer for each. Pay close attention to the object nouns and pronouns you hear in the questions.

1. a. Sí, voy a mandártela.   b. Sí, voy a mandártelos.
2. a. Sí, se lo tengo que hacer.   b. Sí, te lo tengo que hacer.
3. a. Sí, nos los van a traer.   b. Sí, se los voy a traer.
4. a. No, no van a traértelas.   b. No, no van a traérmelas.
5. a. Sí, te las sirvo.   b. Sí, se los sirvo.

B. Cosas de todos los días: El cumpleaños de Gilberto. Practice talking about the surprise birthday party that you gave a friend, using the written cues. When you hear the corresponding number, form sentences using the words provided in the order given, making any necessary changes or additions.

MODELO: (*you see*) 1. (yo) hacerle / una fiesta de sorpresa a Gilberto (*you hear*) uno →
         (*you say*) Le hice una fiesta de sorpresa a Gilberto.

2. venir / muchos de sus amigos
3. Tere / querer venir / pero / no poder
4. todos / traer / o / mandar / regalos
5. Felicia y yo / tener que preparar todo
6. Fernando y Raúl / servir los refrescos
7. Fernando / contar chistes / como siempre
8. todos / divertirse / y / reírse
9. nadie / quejarse
10. Gilberto / tener que bailar / con todas las muchachas
11. ¡(él) / ponerse / muy nervioso!

CAPÍTULO

9

VOCABULARIO Preparación

A. Gustos y preferencias. You will hear a series of descriptions of what people like to do. Each will be said twice. Listen carefully, and circle the letter of the activity or activities that are best suited to each person.

1. a. nadar   b. jugar al ajedrez   c. tomar el sol
2. a. dar fiestas   b. ir al teatro   c. ir a un bar
3. a. ir a un museo   b. hacer *camping*   c. hacer un *picnic*
4. a. pasear en bicicleta b. esquiar   c. correr
5. a. jugar al fútbol   b. ir a un museo   c. ir al cine

B. Las actividades y el tiempo. You will hear a series of descriptions of weather and activities. Write the number of the description next to the corresponding picture. **¡OJO!** Listen carefully. There is an extra description.

a. _____

b. _____

c. _____

d. _____

C. Mandatos para el nuevo robot. Imagine that your family has been chosen to test a model robot in your home. Tell the robot what to do in each of the following situations, using the oral cues. ¡OJO! You will be using **Ud.** command forms.

> MODELO: (*you hear*) uno (*you see*) →
> (*you say*) Lave los platos.

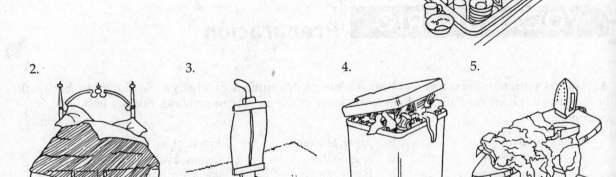

D. ¿Qué están haciendo estas personas? Tell what each person is doing when you hear the corresponding name. Use the present progressive in your answers. (Remember to repeat the correct answer.)

> MODELO: (*you hear*) uno (*you see*) →
> (*you say*) Jorge está lavando las ventanas.

■■■Los hispanos hablan: ¿Cuál es tu pasatiempo favorito?

Paso 1. You will hear two answers to this question. Listen carefully and jot down notes about what each person says. The following words appear in the answers. (Compare your notes to the text in the Appendix.)

los aparadores	*display windows*
los bancos	*soda fountains*
los bancos	*benches*

Xiomara

_____

_____

_____

Gabriela

_____

_____

_____

Paso 2. Now, pause and answer these questions. (Check your answers in the Appendix.)

1. ¿Qué actividades tienen en común las dos jóvenes?

   _____

2. ¿Qué pasatiempos no tienen en común Gabriela y Xiomara?

   _____

Now resume listening.

PRONUNCIACIÓN Y ORTOGRAFÍA *p* and *t*

A. Repeticiones. Like the [k] sound, Spanish **p** and **t** are not aspirated as they are in English. Compare the following pairs of aspirated and nonaspirated English sounds.

   pin / spin   pan / span   tan / Stan   top / stop

Repeat the following words, imitating the speaker.

1. pasar   patinar   programa   puerta   esperar
2. tienda   todos   traje   estar   usted

Now, read the following phrases and sentences after you hear the corresponding number. Repeat the correct pronunciation after the speaker.

3. una tía trabajadora
4. unos pantalones pardos

5. Tomás, toma tu té.
6. Pablo paga el periódico.

B. Repaso: [p], [t], [k]. You will hear a series of words. Each will be said twice. Circle the letter of the word you hear.

1. a. pata   b. bata
2. a. van   b. pan
3. a. coma   b. goma
4. a. dos   b. tos
5. a. de   b. té
6. a. callo   b. gallo

C. Dictado. You will hear four sentences. Each will be said twice. Listen carefully and write what you hear. (Check your answers in the Appendix.)

1. _____
2. _____
3. _____
4. _____

GRAMÁTICA

27. Talking About the Past (Part 4) • Descriptions and Habitual Actions in the Past: Imperfect of Regular and Irregular Verbs

A. Gramática en acción: Los indígenas colombianos

Paso 1. Dictado. You will hear the following paragraph about the indigenous people of Colombia. Listen carefully and write the missing words. (Check your answers in the Appendix.)

Cuando los españoles llegaron al territorio que hoy es Colombia, _____ allí diversos pueblos indígenas que _____ a tres grandes familias.

LOS CHIBCHAS: _____ en los altiplanos y en las zonas frías de los Andes, en el interior. Su organización social _____ _____ en el matriarcado.

LOS CARIBES: _____ la zona costera caribeña. _____ un pueblo guerrero y comerciante.

LOS ARAWACOS: _____ el interior oriental, cerca de los ríos Amazonas, Putumayo y Caquetá. _____ la arquitectura más avanzada de todas las tribus.

Paso 2. ¿Qué recuerda Ud.? Now pause and complete the following sentences with words chosen from the list. There is an extra word in the list. (Check your answers in the Appendix.)

comerciante   interior   arquitectura   altiplanos   diversos

1. _____ pueblos indígenas habitaban lo que hoy es Colombia.

2. Los chibchas vivían en las zonas frías y en los _____.

3. Los caribes, un pueblo _____ y guerrero, vivían en el Caribe.

4. Los arawacos tenían la _____ más avanzada de todos los grupos indígenas.

Now resume listening.

B. Encuesta: ¿Qué hacía Ud. y cómo era cuando era joven? You will hear a series of statements about what you used to do or what you were like when you were younger. For each statement, check the appropriate answer. No answers will be given. The answers you choose should be correct for you!

1. ☐ Sí   ☐ No   4. ☐ Sí   ☐ No   6. ☐ Sí   ☐ No

2. ☐ Sí   ☐ No   5. ☐ Sí   ☐ No   7. ☐ Sí   ☐ No

3. ☐ Sí   ☐ No

C. En el aeropuerto: Una despedida

Paso 1. You will hear a description of a farewell between parents and their son, who is leaving home to attend medical school. Listen carefully, and indicate the appropriate actions for each person. First, pause and look at the chart. (Check your answers in the Appendix before you begin **Paso 2.**)

	ESTAR EN EL AEROPUERTO	IR A SAN JOSÉ	ESTAR MUY NERVIOSO/A	ESTAR PREOCUPADO/A	SENTIRSE TRISTE
Gustavo					
la madre de Gustavo					
el padre de Gustavo					

Paso 2. Now you will hear a series of statements about the passage. Each will be said twice. Circle **C** if the statement is true or **F** if it is false.

1. C F   2. C F   3. C F   4. C F   5. C F

Paso 3. Now answer the questions you hear, based on the information in your chart. Check the answers for **Paso 1** in the Appendix before you begin **Paso 3.** Each question will be said twice. Pause and write the answers.

1. _____

2. _____

3. _____

4. _____

5. _____

D. Describiendo el pasado: En la primaria. Practice telling what you and others used to do in grade school, using the oral and written cues.

> MODELO: (*you see*) (yo)   (*you hear*) jugar mucho → (*you say*) Jugaba mucho.

1. Rodolfo   2. (tú)   3. todos   4. (nosotros)

28. Expressing Extremes • Superlatives

A. Gramática en acción: ¡El número uno! Encuesta. You will hear a series of statements about famous personalities. Indicate what is true, in your opinion, by checking the appropriate answers. No answers will be given. The answers you choose should be correct for you!

	ESTOY DE ACUERDO.	NO ESTOY DE ACUERDO.
1.	☐	☐
2.	☐	☐
3.	☐	☐
4.	☐	☐
5.	☐	☐
6.	☐	☐

B. Las opiniones de Margarita

Paso 1. Apuntes. You will hear a brief paragraph in which Margarita gives her opinions about a variety of topics. Listen carefully and write down her opinions. First, listen to the list of topics. (Check your answers in the Appendix.)

la fiesta más divertida del año: _____

el peor mes del año: _____

la mejor película del mundo: _____

el quehacer doméstico más aburrido: _____

Paso 2. Now pause and express your own opinion about the same topics. No answers will be given. The answers you choose should be correct for you!

En mi opinión...

1. La fiesta más divertida del año es _____

2. El peor mes del año es _____

3. La mejor película del mundo es _____

4. El quehacer doméstico más aburrido es _____

Now resume listening.

C. Sólo lo mejor... Imagine that your friend's **quinceañera** has the best of everything. Answer some questions about it, using the written cues.

MODELO: (*you see and hear*) Los vestidos son elegantes, ¿no? (*you see*) fiesta →
(*you say*) Sí, son los vestidos más elegantes de la fiesta.

1. Antonio es un chico guapo,
   ¿verdad? / fiesta
2. La música es buena, ¿no? / mundo

3. Y la comida, qué rica, ¿no? / mundo
4. La fiesta es divertida, ¿verdad? / año

29. Getting Information (Part 2) • Summary of Interrogative Words

A. Gramática en acción: Un restaurante de Connecticut. You will hear a series of questions about the following ad. Circle the letter of the best response to each. First pause and read the ad.

1. a. El club de baile   b. El pavo real
2. a. New Haven   b. Garvey
3. a. La Orquesta Mala Fe   b. la comida colombiana
4. a. el pavo   b. los mariscos
5. a. sabrosos platos   b. amplio y lujoso
6. a. Son las 11:30 de la mañana. b. A las 11:30 de la mañana.

B. Preguntas y respuestas. You will hear a series of questions. Each will be said twice. Circle the letter of the best answer to each.

1. a. Es de Juan.   b. Es negro.
2. a. Están en México.   b. Son de México.
3. a. Soy alto y delgado.   b. Bien, gracias. ¿Y Ud.?
4. a. Mañana.   b. Tengo cinco.
5. a. Es gris.   b. Tengo frío.
6. a. Con Elvira.   b. Elvira va a la tienda.
7. a. A las nueve.   b. Son las nueve.

C. ¿Qué dijiste? Your friend Eva has just made several statements, but you haven't understood everything she said. You will hear each statement only once. Choose either **¿Qué?** or **¿Cuál?** and form a question to elicit the information you need.

> MODELO: (*you hear*) La capital del Perú es Lima.
> (*you see*) a. ¿qué? b. ¿cuál? →
> (*you say*) b. ¿Cuál es la capital del Perú?

1. a. ¿qué? b. ¿cuál?
2. a. ¿qué? b. ¿cuál?
3. a. ¿qué? b. ¿cuál?
4. a. ¿qué? b. ¿cuál?
5. a. ¿qué? b. ¿cuál?

D. Entrevista con la Srta. Moreno. Interview Ms. Moreno, an exchange student, for your campus newspaper, using the written cues. Add any necessary words. You will hear the correct question, as well as her answer. Use her name only in the first question.

> MODELO: (*you hear*) uno (*you see*). ¿dónde? / ser →
> (*you say*) Srta. Moreno, ¿de dónde es Ud.? (*you hear*) Soy de Chile.

2. ¿dónde? / vivir
3. ¿dónde? / trabajar
4. ¿qué? / idiomas / hablar
5. ¿cuál? / ser / deporte favorito

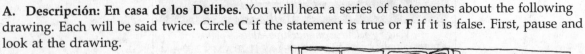

UN POCO DE TODO (Para entregar)

A. Descripción: En casa de los Delibes. You will hear a series of statements about the following drawing. Each will be said twice. Circle **C** if the statement is true or **F** if it is false. First, pause and look at the drawing.

1. C F
2. C F
3. C F
4. C F
5. C F
6. C F

B. *Listening Passage:* **¿Cómo se pasan los fines de semana y los días de fiesta?**

Antes de escuchar. Pause and do the following prelistening exercise.

Before you listen to the passage, read the following statements about how some people spend weekends or holidays. Check those statements that are true for you and your family.

☐ Los fines de semana son ocasiones familiares.

☐ Pasamos los fines de semana o los días de fiesta en nuestra casa en el campo.

☐ Mi madre siempre prepara una comida especial los domingos.

☐ Paso el fin de semana con mis amigos y no con mi familia.

☐ Después de comer, toda la familia sale a dar un paseo por el parque.

☐ Paso el fin de semana con mis abuelos.

Now resume listening.

Listening Passage. Now you will hear a passage about how some Hispanics spend their weekends and holidays. The following words appear in the passage.

adinerados	personas que tienen mucho dinero
a mediodía	*at noon*
se casan	*get married*
el hogar	*home*
el descanso	*rest*
se suele	*it is the custom (to)*
elegir	*to choose, pick*
los columpios	*swings*
los críos	*young children*
charlando	hablando, conversando
relajados	*relaxed*

Después de escuchar. Read the following statements. Circle **C** if the statement is true or **F** if it is false. If the statement is false, according to the passage, correct it.

1. C   F   Muchos hispanos tienen otra casa fuera de la ciudad.

     _____

2. C   F   Normalmente los abuelos no pasan tiempo con sus hijos y nietos.

     _____

3. C   F   Los domingos se almuerza rápidamente para poder ir al cine o al teatro.

     _____

4. C   F   Por lo general, los padres no pasan tiempo con sus hijos durante el fin de semana.

     _____

Now resume listening.

C. Y para terminar… Entrevista. You will hear a series of questions. Each will be said twice. Answer based on your own experience. Pause and write the answers.

1. _____

2. _____

3. _____

4. _____

5. _____

6. _____

VIDEOTECA Minidramas*

Paso 1. La invitación. In the following conversation, Lupe tells Antonio and Juan about a surprise party for Diego. Listen and read along with the speakers. Pay close attention to how Rocío rejects Lupe's invitation, and how Antonio and Juan accept it.

ANTONIO: ¡Hola, Lupe!

LUPE: Hola, Antonio. Oye, ¿está aquí Diego?

ANTONIO: No, no está. ¿Por qué?

LUPE: Ah, muy bien. Pues, el próximo fin de semana le quiero dar una fiesta sorpresa a Diego. Es su cumpleaños. Quiero invitar a todos Uds. a la fiesta.

ANTONIO: ¡Qué padre! ¿Y cuándo es la fiesta? ¿El viernes? ¿El sábado?

LUPE: El sábado. Rocío, ¿te gustaría venir?

ROCÍO: Ay, Lupe, me gustaría mucho, pero no puedo. Ya tengo planes para el sábado. Mis padres vienen al D.F. a visitarme y vamos a ir al Ballet Folklórico esa noche.

JUAN: ¡Qué pena! Pero yo sí voy.

ANTONIO: Y yo también. Gracias por la invitación. ¿Puedo invitar a Mónica y a José Luis también?

LUPE: ¡Claro que sí! ¡Muy bien! Entonces, ¿por qué no vienen a mi casa a las siete? Y por favor, no le vayan a decir nada a Diego.

JUAN: No te preocupes. Él va a estar muy sorprendido.

Paso 2. Aplicación. Now you will participate in two similar conversations, partially printed in your manual, in which you reject and accept invitations. Complete them using the written cues. Here are the cues for your first conversation. You will need to conjugate the verbs.

gracias / pero no poder / tener que estudiar

1. TEODORO: Oye, ¿te gustaría ir al cine el viernes? Dan (*They're showing*) una película buenísima.

    UD.: _____,[1] _____.[2] _____.[3]

    TEODORO: ¡Qué lástima! Tal vez podamos ir el próximo viernes.

Here are the cues for your second conversation. You will also need to conjugate the verbs.

ser una buena idea / a qué hora querer (tú) salir / sí, estar bien

2. CARIDAD: ¿Qué tal si vamos al parque esta tarde y hacemos un *picnic*?

    UD.: ¡_____![1] ¿_____?[2]

    CARIDAD: A las tres, más o menos. ¿Vale? (*O.K.?, Sp.*)

    UD.: _____.[3]

---

*This **Minidramas** videoclip is available on the DVD to accompany *Puntos de partida*, Eighth Edition.

PRUEBA CORTA

A. Recuerdos. You will hear a passage about a person's childhood memories. Then you will hear a series of questions. Circle the letter of the best answer for each.

1. a. Trabajaba en Panamá.   b. Vivía en Panamá.
2. a. Hacía calor.   b. No hacía calor.
3. a. Jugaba béisbol.   b. Patinaba con sus amigos.
4. a. Iba al cine.   b. Iba al centro.
5. a. Patinaba con sus padres.   b. Patinaba con sus amigos.
6. a. Daba paseos en el parque.   b. Daba paseos en el cine.
7. a. Su quehacer favorito era lavar los platos.   b. No le gustaba lavar los platos.

B. Cosas de todos los días: Una niñez feliz. Practice talking about your imaginary childhood, using the written cues. When you hear the corresponding number, form sentences using the words provided in the order given, making any necessary changes or additions.

MODELO: (*you see*) 1. (yo) / ser / niño muy feliz   (*you hear*) uno →
(*you say*) *Era* un niño muy feliz.

2. cuando / (yo) / ser/ niño, / vivir / Colombia
3. mi familia / tener / una casa / bonito / Medellín
4. mi hermana y yo / asistir / escuelas públicas
5. todos los sábados, / mi mamá / ir de compras
6. me / gustar / jugar / con mis amigos
7. los domingos / (nosotros) / reunirse / con / nuestro / abuelos

CAPÍTULO 10

VOCABULARIO Preparación

A. Asociaciones. You will hear a series of activities. Each will be said twice. Circle the body part that you associate with each. ¡OJO! There may be more than one answer for each activity.

1. los pies	las piernas	los dientes	la garganta
2. los pulmones	las manos	la nariz	los ojos
3. los pulmones	la boca	las manos	las piernas
4. los dientes	la garganta	el corazón	la boca
5. los ojos	los pulmones	las piernas	el estómago
6. la nariz	los oídos	las orejas	la garganta

B. Algunas partes del cuerpo. Identify the following body parts when you hear the corresponding number. Use **Es...** or **Son...** and the appropriate definite article.

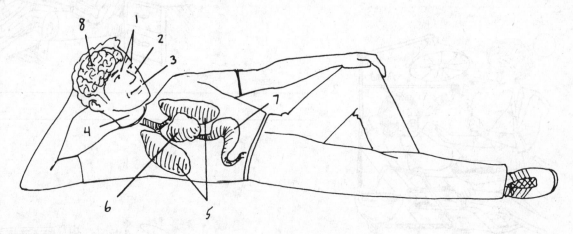

C. Para completar. You will hear a series of incomplete statements. Each will be said twice. Circle the letter of the word or phrase that best completes each statement.

1. a. ponerle una inyección b. respirar bien
2. a. guardamos cama b. nos sacan una muela
3. a. una tos b. un jarabe
4. a. frío b. un resfriado

D. Descripción: Hablando de problemas de salud

Paso 1. In each of the following drawings, a person is suffering from some type of ailment. Pause and write what the ailment is, based on the cues in the drawing. You should also tell where each person might be. The first one is partially done for you. (The small circles are for **Paso 2.** Check your answers to **Paso 1** in the Appendix before you begin **Paso 2.**)

1.

Darío tiene dolor de _____.

(A Darío le duele el _____.)

Él está en _____

2. _____
_____

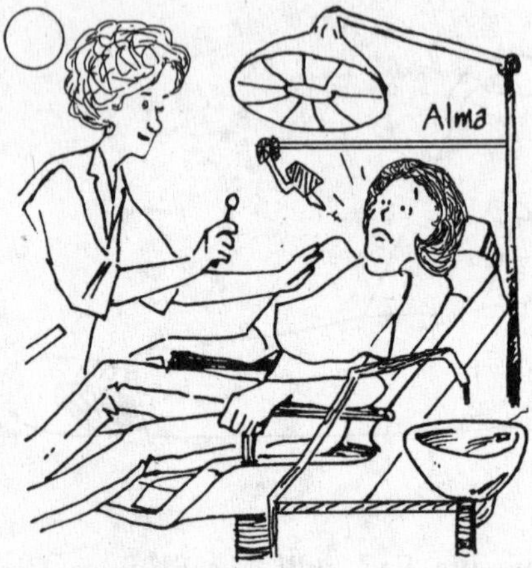

3. _____
_____

4. _____
_____

Now resume listening.

Paso 2. Now you will hear a doctor's recommendations. Each will be said twice. Write the letter of the recommendation in the circle of the corresponding drawing.

■■■Los hispanos hablan: ¿Practicas algún deporte? ¿Por qué?

Paso 1. You will hear several Hispanic students tell about the sports they play and why. The first time you listen, write the name of the sport or sports played by each student. Then, listen again and jot down each person's reasons for choosing the sport. The following words appear in the passages. (Check your answers in the Appendix before you begin **Paso 2**.)

emocionante	*exciting*	habilidad y destreza	*ability and skill*
entretenido	*entertaining, fun*	mantenerse en forma	*to stay in shape*
que uno se engorde	*that one get fat*		

	DEPORTE(S)	RAZÓN POR LA CUAL SE PRACTICA
Clara		
Antonio		
Gabriela		
Patricia		
Teresa		
José		
Xiomara		
Erick		

Paso 2. Now pause and answer these questions, based on the chart. (Check your answers in the Appendix.)

1. ¿Qué deporte es más popular entre los estudiantes que contestaron las preguntas?

   _____

2. ¿Cuántas personas mencionaron entre sus razones la salud o los beneficios para el cuerpo?

   _____

Now resume listening.

PRONUNCIACIÓN Y ORTOGRAFÍA   *s, z, ce,* and *ci*

A. El sonido [s]. The [s] sound in Spanish can be spelled several different ways and has several variants, depending on the country or region of origin of the speaker. Listen to the difference between these pronunciations of the [s] sound in two distinct Spanish-speaking areas of the world.*

Spain:	Vamos a llamar a Susana este lunes.
Latin America:	Vamos a llamar a Susana este lunes.
Spain:	Cecilia siempre cena con Alicia.
Latin America:	Cecilia siempre cena con Alicia.

(Continued on p. 128)

---

*The Latin American variant of the [s] sound is used by most speakers in this audio program.

(Continued from p. 127)

	Spain:	Zaragoza	Zurbarán	zapatería
	Latin America:	Zaragoza	Zurbarán	zapatería

Notice also that in some parts of the Hispanic world, in rapid speech, the [s] sound becomes aspirated at the end of a syllable or word. Listen as the speaker pronounces these sentences.

> ¿Hasta cuándo vas a estar allí?   Les mandamos las cartas.

B. Repeticiones. Repeat the following words, imitating the speaker.

1.	sala	pastel	vaso	años
2.	cerebro	ciencias	piscina	ciudad
3.	corazón	azul	perezoso	zapatos
4.	estación	solución	inyección	situación

Now read the following words, phrases, and sentences after you hear the corresponding number. Repeat the correct pronunciation.

5.	los ojos	8.	unas soluciones científicas
6.	las orejas	9.	No conozco a Luz Mendoza de Pérez.
7.	unas médicas españolas	10.	Los zapatos de Celia son azules.

C. Repaso. You will hear a series of words spelled with **c** or **qu**. Each will be said twice. Circle the letter or letters used to spell each word. ¡ojo! Most of the words will be unfamiliar to you. Concentrate on the sounds you hear.

1. c qu   2. c qu   3. c qu   4. c qu   5. c qu   6. c qu

GRAMÁTICA

30. Narrating in the Past (Part 5) • Using the Preterite and the Imperfect

A. Gramática en acción: Dictado: En el consultorio de la Dra. Méndez. Lola and Manolo's daughter Marta is feeling ill, and Lola takes her to see Dra. Méndez. You will hear the conversation that takes place in the doctor's office. Listen carefully and write the missing words. (Check your answers in the Appendix.) Then you will hear a series of statements about the dialogue. Circle **C, F,** or **ND** (**No lo dice**).

DRA. MÉNDEZ: ¿Cuándo _____ a sentirse mal su hija?

MADRE: Ayer por la tarde. _____ resfriada,

_____ mucho y se _____ de

que le _____ el cuerpo y la cabeza.

DRA. MÉNDEZ: ¿Y le _____ algo de fiebre?

MADRE: Sí. Por la noche le _____ la temperatura

y _____ treinta y ocho grados.

DRA. MÉNDEZ: A ver... Tal vez necesite ponerle una inyección...

1. C F ND   2. C F ND   3. C F ND   4. C F ND

B. Condiciones y acciones: De viaje. You will hear a series of sentences describing conditions. Each will be said twice. Write the number of each condition next to the logical action. First, listen to the list of actions.

a. _____ Por eso llegué tarde al aeropuerto.   d. _____ Por eso pedí un vuelo directo.

b. _____ Por eso pedí asiento en la sección   e. _____ Por eso compré un boleto de ida
         de no fumar.   y vuelta.

c. _____ Por eso lo facturé.

C. ¿Un sábado típico? You will hear a series of sentences that describe Carlos's usual Saturday routine. Form new sentences using the oral cues to talk about what he did *last* Saturday. Begin each sentence with **El sábado pasado...**

   MODELO: (*you see and hear*) Todos los sábados, Carlos se despertaba a las siete.
            (*you hear*) ocho → (*you say*) El sábado pasado, se despertó a las ocho.

1. Todos los sábados, iba al centro comercial.   3. Todos los sábados, visitaba a su madre.
2. Todos los sábados, tomaba té por la   4. Todos los sábados, se acostaba temprano.
   mañana.

D. Descripción. Tell what the following people were doing when you hear the corresponding number. Follow the model. You will hear a possible answer.

   MODELO: (*you hear*) uno   (*you see*) cocinar /
            mientras / poner la mesa →
            (*you say*) Luis cocinaba mientras Paula
            ponía la mesa.

1. cocinar / mientras / poner la mesa

2. leer / cuando / entrar

3. cantar / mientras / tocar el piano

4. llorar / mientras / ponerle una inyección

5. jugar / cuando / pegarle

E. Una decisión difícil

Paso 1. You will hear the following sentences about Laura's decision to leave her hometown. Then, when you hear the cue in parentheses, restate the sentences, changing the italicized verbs to the preterite or imperfect, as appropriate. In each case, you will insert the cue at the beginning of the sentence. In this exercise, you will practice narrating in the past.

> MODELO: (*you see and hear*) *Vivimos* en un pequeño pueblo en las montañas.
> (*you hear*) (de niños) →
> (*you say*) De niños, vivíamos en un pequeño pueblo en las montañas.

1. Mi madre *trabaja* en una panadería (*bakery*). (los martes y los jueves)
2. Mi padre *trabaja* en una tienda de comestibles (*food store*). (todos los días)
3. *Vamos* a la ciudad y *compramos* cosas que no *podemos* encontrar en nuestro pueblo. (con frecuencia)
4. *Consigo* trabajo permanente en la ciudad y *decido* dejar mi pueblo para siempre. (un verano)
5. *Empiezo* a tomar clases de noche en la universidad y *dejo* mi puesto permanente por uno de tiempo parcial. (al año siguiente)
6. Mis padres *están* tristes porque yo no *vivo* con ellos, pero ahora están contentos con mi decisión. (antes)

Paso 2. Answer the questions you hear, based on the preceding story. Each question will be said twice.

1. ... 2. ... 3. ... 4. ...

31. Recognizing *que, quien(es), lo que* • Relative Pronouns

A. Gramática en acción: Tus médicos, tus mejores amigos. You will hear an ad about a group of doctors who serve the Hispanic community. Then you will hear a series of statements. Circle **C** if the statement is true or **F** if it is false. If the information in the statement is not contained in the ad, circle **ND** (**No lo dice**).

La Organización de Médicos Hispanohablantes: Siempre contigo

Tus médicos pueden ser tus mejores amigos.

- Son personas con quienes puedes hablar de TODO.
- Son personas que pueden ayudarte y explicarte TODO lo que tú necesitas saber de tu salud.
- Tienen consultorios que están CERCA de ti.
- Y además, ¡hablan ESPAÑOL!

---

1. C F ND   2. C F ND   3. C F ND   4. C F ND

Nombre _____ Fecha _____ Clase _____

B. La salud es lo que importa

Paso 1. Dictado. You will hear the following paragraph. Listen carefully and write the missing words. (Check your answers in the Appendix.)

¿Sabe Ud. _____ debe hacer para ser saludable

emocionalmente? ¿Vive Ud. la vida _____ debe

vivir? Para estar seguro de _____ necesita para la

salud física, consulte con un doctor en _____ confía.

Pero, para lograr un estado de bienestar mental, hágase estas

preguntas:

- ¿Hay personas con _____ puedo hablar si tengo problemas?

- ¿Qué métodos uso para combatir el estrés _____ me causan los problemas diarios?

Paso 2. Preguntas personales. Now pause and write answers to the following questions. No answers will be given.

1. ¿Sabe Ud. lo que debe hacer para ser saludable emocionalmente?

   _____

2. ¿Vive Ud. la vida que debe vivir?

   _____

3. ¿Hay personas con quienes puede hablar si tiene problemas?

   _____

4. ¿Qué métodos usa para combatir el estrés que le causan los problemas diarios?

   _____

Now resume listening.

C. Apuntes: En el consultorio

Paso 1. Una visita con la doctora. You will hear a brief paragraph describing a visit to the doctor's office. Listen carefully and take notes on a separate sheet of paper, if you wish.

Paso 2. ¿Qué recuerda Ud.? Now pause and provide the following information based on the paragraph. (Check your answers in the Appendix.)

1. lo que tenía la narradora: _____

2. la persona con quien quería hablar: _____

3. lo que le dijo la recepcionista: _____

4. la persona a quien va a llamar la próxima vez que se enferme: _____

Now resume listening.

32. Expressing *each other* (Part 2) • Reciprocal Actions with Reflexive Pronouns

A. Gramática en acción: La amistad.

Paso 1. You will hear a brief passage about friendship. Then you will hear a series of statements. Circle **C** if the statement is true or **F** if it is false. If the information in the statement is not contained in the ad, circle **ND** (**No lo dice**).

1. C F ND   3. C F ND
2. C F ND   4. C F ND

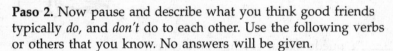

Paso 2. Now pause and describe what you think good friends typically *do*, and *don't* do to each other. Use the following verbs or others that you know. No answers will be given.

VOCABULARIO ÚTIL: ayudarse   hablarse   odiarse (*to hate*)
                             escribirse   llamarse   pelearse (*fight*)

Los buenos amigos _____

_____

Nunca _____

_____

Now resume listening.

B. Descripción: ¿Qué hacen estas personas? Using the written cues, tell what the following pairs of people are doing when you hear the corresponding number. You will be describing reciprocal actions.

1. quererse mucho
2. escribirse con frecuencia
3. darse la mano (*to shake hands*)
4. hablarse por teléfono

UN POCO DE TODO | (Para entregar)

A. En el periódico: La salud

Paso 1. You will hear the following ads from Hispanic newspapers. Listen to them and circle the Spanish words or phrases that express the following. First, pause and scan the list of English words.

DEJE DE FUMAR

1. killers
2. medical treatment
3. a vice

LENTES DE CONTACTO

4. a replacement pair
5. immediate replacement
6. soft or flexible

Paso 2. Now you will hear a series of statements about the ads. Each will be said twice. Circle **C, F,** or **ND (No lo dice)**, according to the ads.

1. C F ND   3. C F ND

2. C F ND   4. C F ND

B. *Listening Passage:* **El sistema médico en los países hispánicos**

Antes de escuchar. Pause and do the following prelistening exercise. Read the following statements about medical systems. Check those that you think apply only to the United States.

1. ☐ El sistema médico está controlado por el gobierno (*government*).

2. ☐ Hay una gran cantidad de compañías de seguro (*insurance companies*).

3. ☐ Hay menos compañías de seguro.

4. ☐ Cada persona paga los gastos médicos de acuerdo con (*according to*) su salario y no de acuerdo con el tipo de seguro que tiene.

5. ☐ Cualquier (*Any*) persona tiene derecho (*right*) al mejor tratamiento médico posible.

6. ☐ Hay muchas personas que no tienen acceso al tratamiento médico, ya sea (*be it*) por falta de dinero o porque no tienen seguro.

7. ☐ A veces, es necesario esperar mucho tiempo para ver al médico.

8. ☐ A veces hay mucha demanda, pero hay pocos servicios y personal disponibles (*available personnel*).

Now resume listening.

Listening Passage. Now you will hear a passage about the medical systems in most of the Hispanic world. The following words and phrases appear in the passage.

proveen	*they provide*
la cobertura	*coverage*
innegables	*undeniable*
la capacidad económica	*economic ability (to pay)*
el impuesto	*tax*
imprescindible	*indispensable*
tiende a disminuir	*tends to diminish or reduce*
el quebradero de cabeza	*problem, something that requires great thought*

Después de escuchar. Indicate whether the following statements are true or false, according to the passage. Correct the false statements.

1. C   F   El sistema médico más común en los países hispanos es el privado.

   _____

2. C   F   El gobierno controla el sistema médico en los Estados Unidos.

   _____

3. C   F   En un sistema de medicina socializada, todos tienen derecho a recibir tratamiento médico.

   _____

4. C   F   Una desventaja de la medicina socializada, especialmente en países menos ricos, es que a veces no hay suficientes servicios médicos o suficientes doctores.

   _____

5. C F El sistema de medicina socializada no diferencia entre los que pagan más y los que pagan menos.

Now resume listening.

C. Y para terminar… Entrevista. You will hear a series of questions. Each will be said twice. Answer based on your own experience. Pause and write the answers.

Hablando de la última vez que estuviste enfermo o enferma

1. _____

2. _____

3. _____

Hablando de la salud en general

4. _____

5. _____

6. _____

VIDEOTECA   Minidramas*

Paso 1. En el consultorio de la Dra. Méndez. In the following conversation, Marta is sick and is being examined by Dra. Méndez. Listen and read along with the speakers.

DRA. MÉNDEZ: ¿Así que no te sientes bien, Marta? Dime lo que te pasa.

MARTA: Anoche me dolió mucho el estómago. Y también la garganta.

MADRE: Sí, y ayer por la tarde estaba muy congestionada.

DRA. MÉNDEZ: ¿Sí? ¿Y cuándo comenzó a sentir estos síntomas?

MADRE: Fue unos días después de que se reunió con su amiga Carolina, quien ya estaba enferma.

DRA. MÉNDEZ: Ajá. Marta, saca la lengua, por favor. Di «ahhh».

MARTA: Ahhh…

DRA. MÉNDEZ: A ver… Respira. Más fuerte. Otra vez.

MADRE: ¿Qué pasa, doctora? ¿Es grave?

DRA. MÉNDEZ: No, no se preocupe. No es nada grave. Lo que tiene es un resfriado. Marta, debes guardar cama durante unos días y tomar muchos líquidos. Sra. Durán, voy a darle dos recetas. Las pastillas son para quitarle la congestión. Y el jarabe se lo puede dar cuando ella tosa.

MADRE: Muy bien, doctora.

DRA. MÉNDEZ: Y debe quedarse en casa algunos días.

MARTA: ¡Estupendo!

MADRE: Marta, por favor…

*This **Minidramas** videoclip is available on the DVD to accompany *Puntos de partida*, Eighth Edition.

Paso 2. Aplicación. Now you will participate in a similar conversation, partially printed in your manual, in which you play the role of a patient. Complete the dialogue using the written cues. You will need to conjugate the verbs. Here are the cues for your conversation. ¡OJO! The cues are not in order.

el lunes pasado   no tener fiebre

estar muy cansado/a   tener dolor de cabeza

DOCTORA: Siéntese, por favor. ¿Qué le ocurre?

UD.: Bueno, _____¹ y

_____.²

DOCTORA: ¿Cuándo empezó a tener estos síntomas?

UD.: _____.³

DOCTORA: Bueno, le voy a tomar la temperatura. Si tiene fiebre, le voy a recomendar que guarde cama por uno o dos días y que tome un antibiótico.

UD.: Y, ¿si _____⁴?

DOCTORA: Entonces le voy a recomendar que tenga paciencia. Es posible que sólo sea un resfriado.

PRUEBA CORTA

A. Consejos para la buena salud. Imagine that you are a doctor and that you are giving advice to one of your patients. Use formal commands based on the oral cues.

MODELO: (*you hear*) hacer ejercicios aeróbicos → (*you say*) Haga ejercicios aeróbicos.

1. ...   2. ...   3. ...   4. ...   5. ...

B. Cosas de todos los días: Una enfermedad muy grave. Practice talking about an event that took place in the past, using the written cues. When you hear the corresponding number, form sentences using the words provided in the order given, making any necessary changes or additions. You will hear the correct answer. ¡OJO! You will be using the preterite or the imperfect forms of the verbs.

MODELO: (*you see*) 1. el mes pasado / (yo) / enfermarse / gravemente   (*you hear*) uno →
(*you say*) El mes pasado *me enfermé* gravemente.

2. estar / en el trabajo / cuando / de repente / (yo) / sentirse muy mal
3. estar / mareado / y / tener / fiebre / muy alta
4. mi jefe (*boss*) / llamar / hospital / inmediatamente
5. ambulancia / llevarme / en seguida / sala de emergencia
6. enfermero / tomarme / temperatura / cuando / entrar / médica
7. tener que / pasar / cuatro días / en el hospital

CAPÍTULO **11**

VOCABULARIO Preparación

A. Descripción: ¡Qué día más terrible! You will hear a series of sentences. Each will be said twice. Write the letter of each sentence next to the appropriate drawing. First, pause and look at the drawings.

1. _____

2. _____

3. _____

4. _____

5. _____

B. Más partes del cuerpo. Identify the following body parts when you hear the corresponding number. Begin each sentence with **Es...** or **Son...** and the appropriate definite article.

C. Presiones de los estudios. Imagine that you have been under a lot of pressure at school and it is affecting your judgment as well as other aspects of your life. Describe what has happened to you, using the oral and written cues.

MODELO: (*you hear*) no pagar   (*you see*) mis cuentas → (*you say*) No pagué mis cuentas.

1. el informe escrito
2. las escaleras
3. el escritorio

4. la pierna
5. un examen

D. Preguntas personales. You will hear a series of questions about how you do certain things. Answer, using the written cues or your own information. You will hear a possible answer. First, listen to the cues.

hablar español	hacer cola	salir con mis amigos
jugar al béisbol	escuchar el estéreo	limpiar la estufa
faltar a clase	tocar el piano	

1. ...   2. ...   3. ...   4. ...

■■■Los hispanos hablan: Describe una superstición común en tu país

You will hear three Hispanic students tell about common superstitions in their respective countries. Take notes as you listen, if you wish. Then check the statements that are true, based on what you heard. The following words appear in the students' answers.

evitan	*avoid*
la escalera	*ladder*
la maldición	*curse*
derramar	*to spill*
campanadas	*tolls (of a bell)*

APUNTES

_____

_____

_____

_____

_____

1. ☐ En los tres países, el gato juega un papel (*plays a role*) en las supersticiones.

2. ☐ En Colombia, es buena suerte derramar sal para el Año Nuevo.

3. ☐ El martes trece es un día de mala suerte en uno de los países mencionados.

4. ☐ Muchas de estas supersticiones son semejantes (*similar*) a las supersticiones estadounidenses.

Now resume listening.

Nombre _____ Fecha _____ Clase _____

PRONUNCIACIÓN Y ORTOGRAFÍA   ñ and ch

A. La letra ñ: Repeticiones. The pronunciation of the letter **ñ** is similar to the sound [ny] in the English words *canyon* and *union*. However, in Spanish it is pronounced as one single sound.

Repeat the following words, imitating the speaker.

1. cana / caña   sonar / soñar   mono / moño   tino / tiño   cena / seña
2. año   señora   cañón   español   pequeña   compañero

Now read the following sentences when you hear the corresponding number. Repeat the correct pronunciation.

3. El señor Muñoz es de España.
4. Los niños pequeños no enseñan español.
5. La señorita Ordóñez tiene veinte años.
6. El cumpleaños de la señora Yáñez es mañana.

B. A escoger. You will hear a series of words. Each will be said twice. Circle the letter of the word you hear.

1. a. pena   b. peña
2. a. una   b. uña
3. a. lena   b. leña
4. a. suena   b. sueña
5. a. mono   b. moño

C. El sonido ch: Repeticiones. In Spanish, when the letters **c** and **h** are combined, they are pronounced like the English *ch* in *church*. Read the following words when you hear the corresponding number, then repeat the correct pronunciation.

1. mucho
2. muchacho
3. Conchita
4. Chile
5. mochila
6. hache

D. Dictado. You will hear five sentences. Each will be said twice. Write what you hear. (Check your answers in the Appendix.)

1. _____
2. _____
3. _____
4. _____
5. _____

GRAMÁTICA

33. Telling How Long Something Has Been Happening or How Long Ago Something Happened • *Hace... que:* Another Use of *hacer*

A. Gramática en acción: ¡Cómo pasa el tiempo!

Paso 1. You will hear the following captions for each drawing.

1. Hace diez años que Marcos enseña en la Universidad de Puerto Rico.

2. Marcos y Esperanza se conocieron hace quince años.

Paso 2. Now pause and write two questions that would elicit the information in each caption. You will be using the expression **¿Cuánto tiempo hace que... ?** (Check your answers in the Appendix.)

1. _____.

2. _____.

Now resume listening.

B. ¿Cuánto tiempo hace... ? Each of the following drawings shows how long something has been going on. Pause and look at the drawings. Then answer the questions. Each will be said twice.

1. ...

2. ...

3. ...

4. ...

C. ¡Felicidades, Arturo y Matilde! You will hear a series of questions about a couple celebrating their 50th wedding anniversary. Answer, using the written cues.

1. 55 años
2. 50 años
3. 48 años
4. 10 años

34. Expressing Unplanned or Unexpected Events • Another Use of *se*

A. Gramática en acción: Un día fatal. You will hear three statements about the following drawings. Write the number of each statement under the correct drawing.

a. _____   b. _____   c. _____

B. Encuesta: ¿Cómo era Ud. en la escuela primaria? You will hear a series of questions about what you were like when you were in grade school. For each question, check the appropriate answer. No answers will be given. The answers you choose should be correct for you!

1. ☐ Sí ☐ No

2. ☐ Sí ☐ No

3. ☐ Sí ☐ No

4. ☐ Sí ☐ No

5. ☐ Sí ☐ No

6. ☐ Sí ☐ No

C. ¡Qué distraído! You will hear a description of Luis, followed by a series of statements about what he forgot to do this morning. Place the number of each statement next to its logical result. First, listen to the results.

a. _____ Va a llegar tarde al trabajo.

b. _____ No va a poder arrancar (*start*) el coche.

c. _____ Es posible que se le queme (*burn down*) el apartamento.

d. _____ Le van a robar la computadora.

e. _____ Lo van a echar (*evict*) de su apartamento.

D. Dictado. You will hear the following sentences. Each will be said twice. Listen carefully and write the missing words. (Check your answers in the Appendix.)

1. A ellos _____ _____ _____ el número de teléfono de Beatriz.

2. A Juan _____ _____ _____ las gafas.

3. Durante nuestro último viaje _____ _____ _____ el equipaje en la estación del tren.

4. A los niños _____ _____ _____ los juguetes (*toys*).

35. ¿*Por o para?* • A Summary of Their Uses

A. Gramática en acción: ¿Qué se representa? You will hear four statements about the following drawings. Write the number of each statement under the correct drawing.

a. _____

b. _____

c. _____

d. _____

B. ¿Qué hacen estas personas? Using **por,** tell what the following people are doing when you hear the corresponding number.

MODELO: (*you hear*) uno (*you see*) 1. hablar / teléfono →
(*you say*) Marcos habla por teléfono.

1. hablar / teléfono

2. viajar / barco

3. caminar / playa

4. correr / parque

5. pagar / 15 dólares / bolígrafos

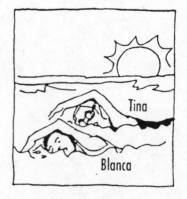

6. nadar / mañana

C. ¿Para qué están Uds. aquí? Using the oral and written cues, tell why the people mentioned are in the locations you hear. Each question will be said twice. First, listen to the list of reasons.

> celebrar nuestro aniversario
>
> descansar y divertirse
>
> hablar con el médico
>
> hacer reservaciones para un viaje a Acapulco
>
> preparar la comida

> MODELO: (*you see*) Armando: Está allí…
> (*you hear*) ¿Para qué está Armando en la cocina? →
> (*you say*) Está allí para preparar la comida.

1. Diana: Está allí…
2. el Sr. Guerra: Está allí…
3. mi esposo/a y yo: Estamos aquí…
4. la familia Aragón: Está allí…

D. La vida diaria. You will hear the following sentences followed by an oral cue. Extend each sentence, using **por** or **para,** as appropriate.

> MODELO: (*you see and hear*) Tengo que mandar los cheques.
> (*you hear*) el miércoles →
> (*you say*) Tengo que mandar los cheques para el miércoles.

1. Salen el próximo mes.
2. Fueron al cine.
3. Estuvo en Honduras.
4. Habla muy bien el inglés.
5. A las ocho vamos a salir.
6. Vendieron su coche viejo.

UN POCO DE TODO | (Para entregar)

A. Situaciones delicadas. You will hear four situations. Choose the best response to each.

1. a. ¡Ay, me hice daño en la mano!
   b. ¡Qué mala suerte, Sr. Ramos! ¿Tiene otro vaso?
   c. Lo siento muchísimo, Sr. Ramos. Fue sin querer. ¿Puedo comprarle otro?
2. a. No me importa que no te guste el menú. Vamos a comer aquí.
   b. Lo siento mucho, pero pensé que te gustaría este restaurante. ¿Quieres ir a otro?
   c. Bueno, yo me quedo aquí, pero si tú quieres irte (*to leave*) a mí no me importa.
3. a. Lo siento, viejo, pero no tengo ganas de trabajar más hoy.
   b. Bueno, si Ud. insiste, me quedo a trabajar.
   c. Solamente voy a trabajar tarde si me da un aumento de sueldo.
4. a. No se preocupe. Estoy bien.
   b. Mire, señor, si sus niños no dejan de hacer tanto ruido, voy a llamar a la policía.
   c. Por favor, señor, dígales a sus niños que no hagan tanto ruido… ¡Tengo un dolor de cabeza tremendo!

B. *Listening Passage:* **Un accidente.** You will hear a conversation between a person who has just had an accident and a person who was on the scene. First, listen to get a general idea of the content. Then go back and listen again for specific information.

Después de escuchar. You will hear a series of questions. Each will be said twice. Not all the questions are based on details of the conversation; some will ask for your opinion. Pause and write the answers. The following words and expressions appear in the questions.

perdió el conocimiento	*became unconscious*
el accidentado	la víctima del accidente
deprimido	*depressed*

1. _____

2. _____

3. _____

4. _____

5. _____

C. Y para terminar… Entrevista. You will hear a series of questions. Each will be said twice. Answer based on your own experience. Pause and write the answers.

1. _____

2. _____

3. _____

4. _____

5. _____

6. _____

VIDEOTECA   Minidramas*

Paso 1. Un día fatal. In the following conversation, José Miguel, his mother, and his grandmother are in the dining room. Listen and read along with the speakers.

JOSÉ MIGUEL:	Bueno, mamá, aquí están las compras del mercado.
ELISA:	¡Ay! ¡José Miguel! ¡Se te cayó todo!
JOSÉ MIGUEL:	Lo siento, mamá. ¡Fue sin querer!
ELISA:	Debes tener más cuidado, hijo.
JOSÉ MIGUEL:	Perdóname. Parece que me levanté con el pie izquierdo hoy. ¡Qué lata!
ELISA:	Ay, no vale la pena molestarte.
MARÍA:	Bueno, pero hay algo bueno en todo esto…
ELISA:	¿Qué es?
MARÍA:	¡Que no llevamos una vida aburrida!

---

*This **Minidramas** videoclip is available on the DVD to accompany *Puntos de partida*, Eighth Edition.

Paso 2. Aplicación. Now you will participate in two conversations, partially printed in your manual, in which you play the role of **Ud.** Complete each conversation using the written cues. Remember to repeat the correct answer. Here are the cues for your conversations. ¡OJO! The cues are not in order.

> Discúlpeme.
>
> No se preocupe.
>
> ¡Lo siento! Fue sin querer.

1. En la farmacia: Ud. se da con una señora y a ella se le cae el frasco (*jar*) de medicina que llevaba.

    SRA.: ¡Ay, no!… ¡el frasco!

    UD.: _____.¹

    SRA.: ¿Qué voy a hacer? Era una medicina para mi hijito, que está enfermo.

    UD.: _____.² Yo le compro otro frasco.

2. En el avión: Ud. se equivoca y toma el asiento de otro pasajero. Cuando la persona vuelve, quiere que Ud. le dé su puesto.

    SR.: Perdón, pero ese es mi asiento.

    UD.: _____.³ Aquí lo tiene.

    SR.: Muchas gracias.

PRUEBA CORTA

A. ¿Cuánto tiempo hace que… ? You will hear a series of questions. Each will be said twice. Answer based on the following chart. ¡OJO! Assume that the current year is 2009. First, pause and look at the chart.

PERSONA(S)	ACTIVIDAD	AÑO EN QUE EMPEZÓ (EMPEZARON) LA ACTIVIDAD
Silvia	trabajar para la universidad	2007
Ernesto	vivir en California	1985
Samuel y Ana	casarse	1997
Laura y su hermana	hacer ejercicios aeróbicos	2003
el Sr. Alvarado	llegar a los Estados Unidos	2004

1. … 2. … 3. … 4. … 5. …

B. Cosas de todos los días: Recuerdos. Practice talking about your friend Benito, using the written cues. When you hear the corresponding number, form sentences using the words provided in the order given, making any necessary changes or additions. ¡OJO! You will be using the preterite or the imperfect forms of the verbs.

MODELO: (*you see*) 1. de niño / Benito / ser / muy torpe   (*you hear*) uno →
(*you say*) De niño, Benito *era* muy torpe.

2. (él) lastimarse / con frecuencia
3. Benito / también / ser / muy distraído
4. frecuentemente / (él) olvidarse de / poner / despertador
5. casi siempre / quedársele / en casa / tarea
6. muchas veces / perdérsele / llaves
7. una vez / (él) caerse / y / romperse / brazo
8. el médico / ponerle / yeso (*cast*)

CAPÍTULO 12

VOCABULARIO   Preparación

A. Hablando de «cositas» (*"a few small things"*). You will hear a brief dialogue between two friends, Lidia and Daniel. Listen carefully and circle the items that are mentioned in their conversation. Don't be distracted by unfamiliar vocabulary. First, pause and look at the drawing.

B. Definiciones. You will hear a series of statements. Each will be said twice. Circle the letter of the word that is defined by each.

1. a. el CD-ROM   b. el control remoto
2. a. el inquilino   b. el alquiler
3. a. la vecindad   b. la vecina
4. a. la jefa   b. el sueldo
5. a. el contestador automático   b. la motocicleta
6. a. el control remoto   b. el / la portero/a
7. a. el primer piso   b. la planta baja

C. Identificaciones. Identify the following items when you hear the corresponding number. Begin each sentence with **Es un...** or **Es una...**

1. ...   2. ...   3. ...   4. ...   5. ...

■■■Los hispanos hablan: Quiero...

Paso 1. Listen to Diana, José, and Karen describe what they want. As you listen to their descriptions, check the appropriate boxes. First, listen to the list of objects. (Check your answers in the Appendix before you begin **Paso 2.**)

	DIANA	JOSÉ	KAREN		DIANA	JOSÉ	KAREN
ropa	☐	☐	☐	un radio portátil	☐	☐	☐
un estéreo	☐	☐	☐	un gran trabajo	☐	☐	☐
cosméticos	☐	☐	☐	un boleto de avión	☐	☐	☐
discos compactos	☐	☐	☐	una grabadora	☐	☐	☐
una guitarra	☐	☐	☐	una batería (*drum set*)	☐	☐	☐
aretes	☐	☐	☐	un ordenador	☐	☐	☐
un auto	☐	☐	☐	una bicicleta	☐	☐	☐

Paso 2. Now, pause and answer the following questions about the descriptions and the chart you completed in **Paso 1.** (Check your answers in the Appendix.)

1. De las tres personas, ¿quién quiere más cosas?

   _____

2. De las tres personas, ¿quién quiere viajar?

   _____

3. ¿Qué cosas desea más de una persona?

   _____

Now resume listening.

PRONUNCIACIÓN Y ORTOGRAFÍA *y and ll*

A. El sonido [y]. At the beginning of a word or syllable, the Spanish sound [y] is pronounced somewhat like the letter *y* in English *yo-yo* or *papaya*. However, there is no exact English equivalent for this sound. In addition, there are variants of the sound, depending on the country of origin of the speaker.

Listen to these differences.

el Caribe: Yolanda lleva una blusa amarilla. Yo no.

España: Yolanda lleva una blusa amarilla. Yo no.

la Argentina: Yolanda lleva una blusa amarilla. Yo no.

B. El sonido [ly]. Although **y** and **ll** are pronounced exactly the same by most Spanish speakers, in some regions of Spain **ll** is pronounced like the [ly] sound in *million,* except that it is one single sound.

Listen to these differences.

> España: Guillermo es de Castilla.
>
> Sudamérica: Guillermo es de Castilla.

C. Repeticiones. Repeat the following words, imitating the speaker.

1. llamo	llueve	yogurt	yate (*yacht*)	yanqui	yoga
2. ellas	tortilla	millón	mayo	destruyo (*I destroy*)	tuyo (*yours*)

D. ¿Ll o l? You will hear a series of words. Each will be said twice. Circle the letter used to spell each.

1. ll l   2. ll l   3. ll l   4. ll l   5. ll l   6. ll l

E. Repaso: ñ, l, ll, y: Dictado. You will hear three sentences. Each will be said twice. Write what you hear. (Check your answers in the Appendix.)

1. _____

2. _____

3. _____

GRAMÁTICA

36. Influencing Others (Part 2) • *Tú* (Informal) Commands

A. Gramática en acción: Mandatos de la adolescencia: Dictado. You will hear a series of statements containing commands. Listen carefully and write the missing words. (Check your answers in the Appendix.)

1. _____ la ropa limpia en tu cómoda.

2. _____ la ropa sucia en el cesto.

3. _____ esos pantalones para ir a la escuela.

4. _____ los zapatos por todas partes.

5. _____ el GameBoy ahora mismo.

6. ¡_____ el iPod! Te estoy hablando.

B. Encuesta: ¿Qué le decían sus padres? You will hear a series of commands that your parents may or may not have given to you when you were a child. For each command, check the appropriate answer. No answers will be given. The answers you choose should be correct for you!

MANDATOS AFIRMATIVOS

1. ☐ Sí ☐ No   3. ☐ Sí ☐ No

2. ☐ Sí ☐ No   4. ☐ Sí ☐ No

MANDATOS NEGATIVOS

5. ☐ Sí ☐ No   7. ☐ Sí ☐ No

6. ☐ Sí ☐ No   8. ☐ Sí ☐ No

C. La vida doméstica de la Cenicienta (*Cinderella*). Play the role of the stepmother and tell Cinderella what she has to do before she can go to the ball. Use affirmative informal commands for the infinitives you will hear.

1. ... 2. ... 3. ... 4. ... 5. ...

D. ¡No lo hagas! Imagine that you are a parent of the child depicted in the drawings. When you hear the corresponding number, tell her *not* to do the things she is doing in each drawing. Use negative informal commands. You will hear a possible answer.

MODELO: (*you hear*) uno   (*you see*) 1. pegarle / Isabel →
                 (*you say*) No le pegues a Isabel.

Isabel

1. pegarle / Isabel

2. saltar (*to jump*) / cama

3. poner / mesa

4. pasear / calle

5. jugar / tantos videojuegos   6. escribir / pared

37. Expressing Subjective Actions or States • Present Subjunctive (Part 1): An Introduction

A. Gramática en acción: La compra de una nueva cámara digital. You will
hear the advice that a father gives to his daughter regarding the purchase of
her first digital camera. Then you will hear a series of statements about the
advice. Circle **C, F,** or **ND** (**No lo dice**).

1. C F ND   3. C F ND

2. C F ND   4. C F ND

B. Encuesta: Hablando de la tecnología. You will hear a series of statements about technology. For
each statement, check the appropriate answer. No answers will be given. The answers you choose
should be correct for you!

1. ☐ Sí   ☐ No   ☐ No tengo opinión.

2. ☐ Sí   ☐ No   ☐ No tengo opinión.

3. ☐ Sí   ☐ No   ☐ No tengo opinión.

4. ☐ Sí   ☐ No   ☐ No tengo opinión.

5. ☐ Sí   ☐ No   ☐ No tengo opinión.

6. ☐ Sí   ☐ No   ☐ No tengo opinión.

C. ¿Qué quiere Arturo?

Paso 1. You will hear Arturo talk about what he wants his siblings to do. Listen to what he says, and complete the following chart by checking the thing he wants each sibling to do or not to do. (Check your answers in the Appendix before you begin **Paso 2.**)

PERSONA	NO JUGAR «NINTENDO»	NO USAR SU COCHE	PRESTARLE SU CÁMARA	BAJAR EL VOLUMEN DEL ESTÉREO
su hermana				
su hermano menor				
sus hermanitos				

Paso 2. Now answer the questions you hear, based on the completed chart. Each question will be said twice.

    1. ...   2. ...   3. ...   4. ...

D. ¿Qué quieren? Answer the following questions using the oral cues.

    1. ¿Qué quiere la jefa (*boss*)?

        MODELO: (*you hear*) Sara → (*you say*) Quiere que Sara llegue a tiempo.

    a. ...   b. ...   c. ...   d. ...

    2. ¿Qué quieres que haga Juan?

        MODELO: (*you hear*) comer ahora → (*you say*) Quiero que Juan coma ahora.

    a. ...   b. ...   c. ...   d. ...

38. Expressing Desires and Requests • Use of the Subjunctive (Part 2): Influence

A. Gramática en acción: ¿Qué quieres que haga yo (*me to do*)**?** You will hear a series of statements. Write the letter of each statement under the corresponding drawing. Careful! There is one extra statement.

1. _____   2. _____   3. _____

B. Presiones de la vida moderna

Paso 1. You will hear a brief paragraph in which Margarita describes her job and what she doesn't like about it. Listen carefully and take notes on a separate sheet of paper.

Paso 2. ¿Qué recuerda Ud.? Now pause and complete the following sentences based on the passage and your notes. Use phrases from the list. Be sure to use the correct present subjunctive form of the verbs. (Check your answers in the Appendix.)

equivocarse	tener teléfono celular
ser más flexible	trabajar los fines de semana
solucionar sus problemas	

1. Los clientes quieren que Margarita _____ técnicos.

2. Su jefa no quiere que ella _____.

3. Margarita quiere que su horario _____.

4. A veces, es necesario que Margarita _____.

5. Margarita prefiere que su coche no _____.

Now resume listening.

C. ¿Qué recomienda el nuevo jefe?

Imagine that you have a new boss in your office, and he is determined to make some changes. When you hear the corresponding numbers, tell what he recommends, using the written cues.

MODELO: (*you hear*) uno (*you see*) 1. El jefe recomienda... Ud. / buscar otro trabajo →
(*you say*) El jefe recomienda que Ud. busque otro trabajo.

2. El jefe recomienda... yo / copiar el contrato
3. El jefe insiste en... todos / trabajar hasta muy tarde
4. El jefe prohíbe... Federico / dormir en la oficina
5. El jefe sugiere... tú / aprender a manejar tu computadora

D. Antes del viaje: ¿Qué quiere Ud. que hagan estas personas?

Imagine that you are a tour leader traveling with a large group of students. Using the oral and written cues, tell each person what you want him or her to do. Begin each sentence with **Quiero que...** , as in the model.

MODELO: (*you hear*) hacer las maletas (*you see*) Uds. →
(*you say*) Quiero que Uds. hagan las maletas.

1. Toño 2. (tú) 3. Ana y Teresa 4. todos 5. todos

A. Descripción: Una familia de la era de la tecnología

Paso 1. You will hear five brief descriptions. Write the letter of each description next to the drawing that it describes. ¡OJO! Not all the drawings will be described. First, pause and look at the drawings.

1. _____   2. _____   3. _____

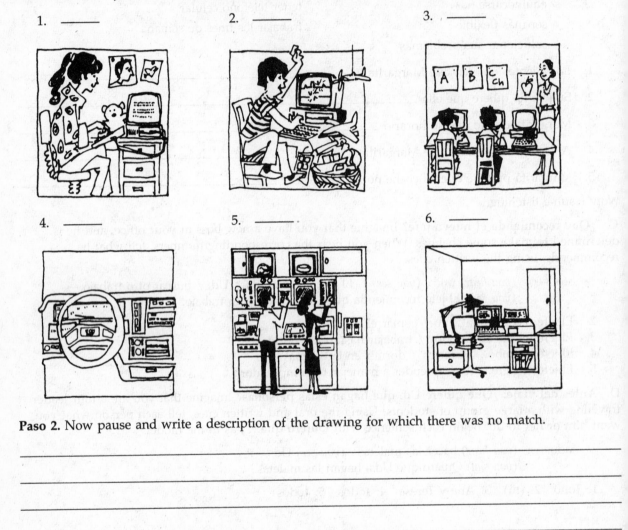

4. _____   5. _____   6. _____

Paso 2. Now pause and write a description of the drawing for which there was no match.

_____

_____

_____

_____

_____

_____

Now resume listening.

B. *Listening Passage:* **Recuerdos de España**

Antes de escuchar. Pause and do the following prelistening exercises.

Answer these questions about Spain to see how much you already know about this European country.

1. ¿Cómo piensa Ud. que es el nivel de vida (*standard of living*) en España?

_____

2. ¿Cree Ud. que España ha cambiado (*has changed*) mucho en los últimos treinta años?

_____

3. ¿Sabe Ud. lo que es la Unión Europea? España pertenece (*belongs*) a ella desde 1986.

_____

4. ¿Cuántas semanas de vacaciones le dan al año si trabaja en los Estados Unidos? ¿Y en España?

_____

Now resume listening.

Listening Passage. Now you will hear a passage in which a person from Spain tells us about his homeland. The following words appear in the passage.

a finales de	*at the end of*	occidental	*western*
en vías de desarrollo	*developing*	con eficacia	*efficiently*
a nivel	*at the level*	los medios	*means*
las cuestiones	*matters*	el ascenso	*promotion*
incluso	*even*	me he americanizado	*I have become Americanized*

Después de escuchar. Pause and check all the statements that, according to the speaker of the passage, describe present-day Spain.

1. ☐ España es un país en vías de desarrollo.

2. ☐ El nivel de vida en las ciudades grandes es bueno.

3. ☐ A los españoles no les gusta trabajar.

4. ☐ Es normal que los españoles tengan cuatro semanas de vacaciones al año.

5. ☐ Las universidades españolas tienen un mejor sistema de bibliotecas que las norteamericanas.

6. ☐ España es un país moderno y desarrollado.

7. ☐ La Unión Europea ha beneficiado (*has benefitted*) a España.

Now resume listening.

C. Y para terminar… Entrevista. You will hear a series of questions. Each will be said twice. Answer based on your own experience. Pause and write the answers.

1. _____
2. _____
3. _____
4. _____
5. _____
6. _____

VIDEOTECA   Minidramas*

Paso 1. Buscando una computadora. In the following conversation, José Miguel and Gustavo talk to a salesperson about computers. Listen and read along with the speakers.

VENDEDORA:	Buenas tardes. ¿En qué les puedo atender?
JOSÉ MIGUEL:	Buenas tardes. Leímos su anuncio en el periódico. Quisiéramos ver las computadoras.
VENDEDORA:	¿Qué modelo buscan? Tenemos varios aquí. Este es nuevo. Viene con monitor, ratón ergonómico y un módem interno.
JOSÉ MIGUEL:	Pero, no tiene lector de CD-ROM interno, ¿verdad? Prefiero uno que lo tenga.
VENDEDORA:	Ese modelo allí tiene lector de CD-ROM interno. Venga. Esta es la mejor de las que tienen CD-ROM.
JOSÉ MIGUEL:	¿Qué te parece, Gustavo?
GUSTAVO:	No está mal… ¿Tiene suficiente memoria para navegar por el Internet?
VENDEDORA:	Sí.
GUSTAVO:	¿Y se puede utilizar también un *browser* de páginas o programas de multimedia?
VENDEDORA:	Este modelo es ideal para multimedia. Y lleva incluidos los programas necesarios para navegar la red.
JOSÉ MIGUEL:	Ah, muy bien, porque pienso utilizar el Internet para ayudarme con mis trabajos en la universidad…

---

*This **Minidramas** videoclip is available on the DVD to accompany *Puntos de partida*, Eighth Edition.

Paso 2. Aplicación. In the preceding conversation, José Miguel and Gustavo were shopping for a computer. It is also important to know how to arrange for repairs once you've bought one! Complete the following dialogue using the written cues. You will play the role of the client. Here are the cues for your conversation. ¡OJO! The cues are not in order.

> va a estar lista (*ready*)
>
> muy buenas
>
> mi computadora no funciona
>
> es una marca (*brand*) nacional

DEPENDIENTE: Buenas tardes. ¿En qué puedo servirle?

CLIENTE: _____.¹ _____.²

DEPENDIENTE: ¿La compró Ud. aquí?

CLIENTE: No, pero _____.³

DEPENDIENTE: En ese caso no hay problema. Se la arreglamos en seguida.

CLIENTE: Muchas gracias. ¿Cuándo _____⁴?

DEPENDIENTE: Dentro de (*Within*) dos días.

PRUEBA CORTA

A. Una oficina con problemas. You are the boss of a large office with an unruly staff that is on the verge of a strike. You will hear what they do not want to do. Tell them what you would like them to do, using the written and oral cues.

> MODELO: (*you hear*) No queremos mandar los documentos. (*you see*) querer →
> (*you say*) Pues, yo quiero que Uds. los manden.

1. recomendar
2. sugerir
3. querer
4. querer
5. mandar

B. Los mandatos de la niñera (*baby-sitter*). Imagine that you are Tito's baby-sitter. Tell him what to do or what not to do, using the oral cues. ¡OJO! You will be using **tú** commands in your sentences.

> MODELO: (*you hear*) sentarse en el sofá → (*you say*) Tito, siéntate en el sofá.

1. ...   2. ...   3. ...   4. ...   5. ...   6. ...

CAPÍTULO **13**

VOCABULARIO **Preparación**

A. Encuesta. You will hear a series of questions. Check the appropriate boxes. No answers will be given. The answers you choose should be correct for you!

1. ☐ Sí   ☐ No   5. ☐ Sí   ☐ No

2. ☐ Sí   ☐ No   6. ☐ Sí   ☐ No

3. ☐ Sí   ☐ No   7. ☐ Sí   ☐ No

4. ☐ Sí   ☐ No   8. ☐ Sí   ☐ No

B. Identificaciones. You will hear a series of words. Write the number of each word next to the item the word describes. First, pause and look at the drawings.

C. Definiciones. You will hear a series of definitions. Each will be said twice. Circle the letter of the word that is defined by each.

1. a. el bailarín   b. el cantante   4. a. la escultora   b. el dramaturgo
2. a. la arquitecta   b. la aficionada   5. a. la compositora   b. el guía
3. a. el músico   b. la ópera   6. a. el poeta   b. el artista

D. Descripción: ¿En qué piso? You will be asked to tell on what floor a number of families live or on which floor businesses are located. Each question will be said twice. Answer, based on the following drawing. First, pause and look at the drawing.

1. ...

2. ...

3. ...

4. ...

5. ...

= 6

= 5

= 4

= 3

= 2

= 1

la planta baja

E. Poniendo las cosas en orden

Paso 1. You will hear a series of questions. Each will be said twice. Circle the correct answer.

1. febrero   enero   junio   abril

2. julio   agosto   octubre   diciembre

3. lunes   jueves   sábado   martes

4. Michael Jordan   Rosie O'Donnell   Neil Armstrong   Antonio Banderas

Paso 2. Now pause and write a sentence, using ordinal numbers, about each of the answers you circled. Number four is done for you. (Check your answers in the Appendix.)

1. _____

2. _____

3. _____

4. _La primera persona que caminó en la luna fue Neil Armstrong._ _____

Now resume listening.

■■■Los hispanos hablan: Dinos algo acerca de la ciudad donde vives

Paso 1. First, pause and check the statements that are true for the city or town in which you live.

1. ☐ Muchas personas viven en el centro de la ciudad.

2. ☐ Hay muchas partes antiguas (*old*).

3. ☐ La mayoría de los teatros, museos, tiendas, etcétera, se encuentran en el centro.

4. ☐ Es normal que la gente esté en las calles hasta muy tarde.

5. ☐ Hay metro (*subway*).

6. ☐ Hay mucha vida cultural.

7. ☐ Es normal que la gente camine en vez de (*instead of*) usar el coche.

Now resume listening.

Paso 2. Pause and check the statements that are true, according to the passage.

1. ☐ Clara nació en Madrid.

2. ☐ Madrid es una ciudad cosmopolita.

3. ☐ Si uno vive en Madrid, es absolutamente necesario tener coche.

4. ☐ En Madrid, es normal que la gente esté en las calles hasta muy tarde.

5. ☐ Es común que mucha gente viva en el centro de la ciudad.

6. ☐ La mayoría de las actividades culturales se encuentran en el centro.

Now resume listening.

PRONUNCIACIÓN Y ORTOGRAFÍA *x* and *n*

A. La letra *x*. The letter x is usually pronounced [ks], as in English. Before a consonant, however, it is often pronounced [s]. Repeat the following words, imitating the speaker.

1.	[ks]	léxico	sexo	axial	existen	examen
2.	[s]	explican	extraordinario	extremo	sexto	extraterrestre

Read the following sentences when you hear the corresponding numbers. Repeat the correct pronunciation.

3. ¿Piensas que existen los extraterrestres?
4. ¡Nos explican que es algo extraordinario!
5. No me gustan las temperaturas extremas.
6. La medicina no es una ciencia exacta.

B. La letra *n*. Before the letters **p, b, v,** and **m,** the letter **n** is pronounced [m]. Before the sounds [k], [g], and [x], **n** is pronounced like the [ng] sound in the English word *sing*. In all other positions, **n** is pronounced as it is in English. Repeat the following words and phrases, imitating the speaker.

1. [m]   convence   un beso   un peso   con Manuel   con Pablo   en Venezuela
2. [ng]   encontrar   conjugar   son generosos   en Quito   en Granada   con Juan

Read the following phrases and sentences when you hear the corresponding numbers. Repeat the correct pronunciation.

3. en Perú
4. son jóvenes
5. con Gloria
6. en México
7. En general, sus poemas son buenos.
8. Los museos están en Caracas.

GRAMÁTICA

39. Expressing Feelings • Use of the Subjunctive (Part 3): Emotion

A. Gramática en acción: Diego y Lupe oyen tocar a los mariachis. You will hear a dialogue in which Diego and Lupe discuss mariachi music. Then you will hear a series of statements. Circle the letter of the person who might have made each statement.

1. a. Lupe   b. Diego   3. a. Lupe   b. Diego
2. a. Lupe   b. Diego   4. a. Lupe   b. Diego

B. El día de la función (*show*). Tell how the following people feel, using the oral and written cues.

MODELO: (*you hear*) el director   (*you see*) temer que / los actores / olvidar sus líneas →
(*you say*) El director teme que los actores olviden sus líneas.

1. esperar que / los actores / no enfermarse
2. temer que / la actriz / estar muy nerviosa
3. temer que / los otros actores / no llegar a tiempo
4. esperar que / la obra / ser buena
5. tener miedo de que / la obra / ser muy larga

C. Descripción: Esperanzas (*Hopes*) **y temores** (*fears*). You will hear two questions about each drawing. Answer, based on the drawings and the written cues.

1. sacar (*to get*) malas notas (*grades*) / sacar una «A»

2. funcionar su computadora / no funcionar su computadora

3. haber regalos para él / no haber nada para él

40. Expressing Uncertainty • Use of the Subjunctive (Part 4): Doubt and Denial

A. Gramática en acción: El traje tradicional de las mujeres indígenas bolivianas. You will hear a brief description of the traditional clothing of indigenous Bolivian women. Then you will see a series of statements about the description. First listen to the following list of words.

la vestimenta (la ropa)   el vuelo (*flare, flounce*)

1. C F Es verdad que hay muchas personas de origen indígena en Bolivia.

2. C F Es dudoso que las mujeres indígenas lleven pantalones.

3. C F Es probable que los sombreros de hongo sean parte de la ropa tradicional de los incas.

4. C F Es seguro que la ropa tradicional indígena ofrece (*offers*) protección contra los rayos solares y el frío.

Now pause and circle **C** or **F,** based on the description.

Now resume listening.

B. ¿Cierto o falso?

Paso 1. Encuesta. You will hear a series of statements. Tell whether each statement is true or false. Answer based on your own experience. No answers will be given. The answers you give should be correct for you!

1. ☐ No es cierto que me encante.   ☐ Es cierto que me encanta.

2. ☐ No es cierto que lo tenga.   ☐ Es cierto que lo tengo.

3. ☐ No es cierto que lo prefiera.   ☐ Es cierto que lo prefiero.

4. ☐ No es cierto que conozca a uno.   ☐ Es cierto que conozco a uno.

5. ☐ No es cierto que sea aficionado/a.   ☐ Es cierto que soy aficionado/a.

Paso 2. Para completar. Now pause and complete the following sentences based on your own preferences.

1. Es cierto que me encanta(n) _____

2. No es cierto que me encante(n) _____

3. Es cierto que tengo _____

4. No es cierto que tenga _____

5. Es cierto que soy aficionado/a al / a la _____

6. No es cierto que sea aficionado/a al / a la _____

Now resume listening.

C. ¿Qué piensa Ud.? Imagine that your friend Josefina has made a series of statements. Respond to each, using the written cues. You will hear each one twice. ¡OJO! You will have to use the indicative in some cases.

MODELO: (*you hear*) Anita va al teatro esta noche.   (*you see*) No creo que... →
(*you say*) No creo que Anita vaya al teatro esta noche.

1. No creo que...
2. Dudo que...
3. Es imposible que...
4. Es verdad que...
5. Estoy seguro/a de que...

D. Observaciones. You will hear a series of statements about the following drawings. Each will be said twice. React to each statement, according to the model. Begin each answer with **Es verdad que...** or **No es verdad que...**

MODELO: (*you hear*) Amalia tiene un auto nuevo. →
(*you say*) No es verdad que Amalia tenga un
auto nuevo.

Amalia

1.

2.

3.

4.

5.

41. Expressing Influence, Emotion, Doubt, and Denial • The Subjunctive (Part 5): A Summary

A. Gramática en acción: Los tejidos de Otavalo, Ecuador: Dictado. You will hear a series of statements about the traditional crafts of Otavalo, Ecuador. Listen carefully and write the missing words. (Check your answers in the Appendix.)

1. Algún día _____ _____ el famoso mercado de Otavalo en el Ecuador.

2. _____ que el mercado _____ en las montañas del Ecuador.

3. No me _____ que _____ mucho turismo porque es una zona muy bonita.

4. _____ que los otavaleños _____ hermosos tejidos.

5. _____ que los otavaleños no _____ sus ricas tradiciones.

B. Se venden coches nuevos y usados. You will hear three ads for automobiles. Listen and complete the following sentences by writing the number of the ad in the appropriate space. First, pause and read the incomplete statements. (Check your answers in the Appendix.)

a. Dudo que el coche del anuncio número _____ sea una ganga.

b. El auto del anuncio número _____ es un auto pequeño y económico.

c. Es probable que el coche del anuncio número _____ gaste mucha gasolina.

Now resume listening.

C. ¿Qué quiere Ud. que hagan estas personas? You will hear a series of questions. Answer, using an appropriate written cue.

MODELO: (*you hear*) ¿Qué quiere Ud. que haga el profesor? →
(*you say*) Quiero que no nos dé un examen.

explicarme las obras de arte
mostrarme el lector de DVD
no darnos un examen
tomarme la temperatura
traerme la ensalada

1. ...   2. ...   3. ...   4. ...

UN POCO DE TODO | (Para entregar)

A. En un museo. You will hear a dialogue in which a museum guide explains Pablo Picasso's famous painting, *Guernica,* to some visitors. You will also hear two of the visitors' reactions to the painting. Then you will hear a series of statements. Circle **C, F,** or **ND** (**No lo dice**).

1. C F ND　　2. C F ND　　3. C F ND　　4. C F ND

B. *Listening Passage:* Primeras impresiones

Antes de escuchar. You will hear a passage in which a person who is now living in this country tells about her first impressions of people in the United States. The following words and phrases appear in the passage.

las amistades	los amigos	echo de menos	*I miss*
aumentó	*increased*	el pueblo	*people*
judía	*Jewish*	demuestra	*shows*
para que yo pudiera	*so that I could*	nos besamos	*we kiss each other*
maravillosa	*marvelous, wonderful*	(nos) abrazamos	*we hug (each other)*
para que yo tuviera	*so that I would have*		

Listening Passage. Here is the passage. First, listen to it to get a general idea of the content. Then go back and listen again for specific information.

Después de escuchar. Circle the best answer to each of the following questions. ¡OJO! There may be more than one answer for some items.

1. Es probable que la persona que habla sea de...
   a. España.　　b. los Estados Unidos.　　c. Latinoamérica.　　d. Nueva York.
2. Al principio (*beginning*), esta persona pensaba que los estadounidenses eran...
   a. abiertos.　　b. perezosos.　　c. fríos.　　d. contentos.
3. La amiga que invitó a esta persona a su casa era...
   a. protestante.　　b. judía.　　c. ateísta.　　d. católica.
4. Antes de visitar a la familia de Abi, la narradora...
   a. no conocía Nueva York.
   b. compró regalos.
   c. pasaba la Navidad con su familia.
   d. no sabía mucho de las tradiciones judías.
5. La familia de Abi no entendía...
   a. español.
   b. la tradición de Navidad.
   c. por qué se dan regalos el seis de enero.
   d. por qué la narradora no tenía muchos amigos.
6. Ahora, la estudiante hispánica piensa que...
   a. los estadounidenses son gente fría.
   b. los estadounidenses no se besan lo suficiente.
   c. los estadounidenses no saben nada de las tradiciones hispánicas.
   d. los estadounidenses demuestran el cariño de una manera distinta de la de los hispanos.

Now resume listening.

C. Y para terminar… Entrevista. You will hear a series of questions. Each will be said twice. Answer based on your own experience. Pause and write the answers.

1. _____
2. _____
3. _____
4. _____
5. _____
6. _____

VIDEOTECA Minidramas*

Paso 1. Hablando del arte. In this conversation, Diego and Lupe are talking about art preferences. Listen and read along with the speakers.

DIEGO: ¿Ya sabes sobre qué vas a escribir tu trabajo para la clase de arte?

LUPE: Creo que sí. Me interesan mucho el arte y la vida de Frida Kahlo, así que voy a escribir algo sobre ella.

DIEGO: Kahlo pintó muchos autorretratos, ¿no?

LUPE: Sí, y sus autorretratos siempre tienen elementos simbólicos que representan sus emociones y su estado de ánimo. Sus cuadros me gustan muchísimo. Su esposo fue Diego Rivera, uno de los muralistas más famosos de México. Mira. Aquí ves uno de sus cuadros.

DIEGO: Conozco varios murales de Rivera. Los vi en el Palacio Nacional. Pero a mí me impresionan más los murales de José Clemente Orozco.

LUPE: Sí, Orozco fue un muralista excelente. Mira. Aquí ves uno de sus cuadros.

DIEGO: Así que vas a escribir sobre Frida Kahlo. ¿Qué más te interesa sobre ella?

LUPE: Bueno, me interesa mucho su arte, claro. Pero también me interesa porque llevó una vida muy difícil. Sufrió mucho, pero nunca dejó de apreciar la belleza de vivir…

Paso 2. Aplicación. Now you will participate in a similar conversation, partially printed in your manual, in which you play the role of **Ud.** Complete it using the written cues. You will need to conjugate the verbs. Here are the cues for your conversation. ¡OJO! The cues are not in order.

> haber entradas
>
> ir (nosotros) a un concierto de música clásica
>
> ser más emocionante

SU AMIGA: ¿Qué tal si vamos a un concierto este fin de semana? Hace tiempo que no vamos.

UD.: Está bien, pero esta vez prefiero que _____.[1]

SU AMIGA: Bueno, si insistes. Pero, ¿por qué te gusta tanto ese tipo de música?

UD.: Me gusta porque creo que _____.[2]

SU AMIGA: Bueno, hay un concierto de Beethoven el sábado a las ocho. ¿Qué te parece?

UD.: ¡Perfecto! Ojalá que todavía _____.[3]

---

*This **Minidramas** video clip is available on the DVD to accompany *Puntos de partida*, Eighth Edition.

PRUEBA CORTA

A. Apuntes. You will hear a brief paragraph that tells about a new museum that is opening soon. Listen carefully and, while listening, write the information requested. Write all numbers as numerals. First, listen to the requested information. (Check your answers in the Appendix.)

El nombre del museo: _____

El tipo de arte que se va a exhibir: _____

La fecha en que se va a abrir el museo: _____

El nombre del director del museo: _____

La hora de la recepción: _____

¿Es necesario hacer reservaciones? _____

¿Va a ser posible hablar con algunos de los artistas? _____

B. Cosas de todos los días: Se buscan bailarines. Practice talking about dance director Joaquín Cortés's search for new dancers for his dance troupe, using the written cues. When you hear the corresponding number, form sentences using the words provided in the order given, making any necessary changes or additions. ¡ojo! You will need to make changes to adjectives and add articles, if appropriate.

MODELO: (*you see*) 1. Joaquín / insistir en / que / bailarines / tener / mucho / experiencia
(*you hear*) uno →
(*you say*) Joaquín *insiste* en que *los* bailarines *tengan mucha* experiencia.

2. él / querer / que / bailarines / ser / atlético
3. también / ser / necesario / que / (ellos) saber / cantar / música / flamenco
4. es cierto / que / Joaquín / ser / muy / exigente
5. Joaquín / temer / que / no / poder / encontrarlos / pronto
6. ¡ojalá / que / bailarines / desempeñar / bien / papeles!

CAPÍTULO 14

VOCABULARIO   Preparación

A. ¿Qué opina sobre el medio ambiente? You will hear a series of statements about environmental concerns. Express your opinion about the issues by checking the appropriate boxes. No answers will be given. The answers you choose should be correct for you!

	SÍ ENFÁTICO	SÍ	NO TENGO OPINIÓN	NO	NO ENFÁTICO
1.	☐	☐	☐	☐	☐
2.	☐	☐	☐	☐	☐
3.	☐	☐	☐	☐	☐
4.	☐	☐	☐	☐	☐
5.	☐	☐	☐	☐	☐
6.	☐	☐	☐	☐	☐

B. Los animales

Paso 1. Descripción. Identify the following animals when you hear the corresponding number. Begin each sentence with **Es un... , Es una... ,** or **Son...**

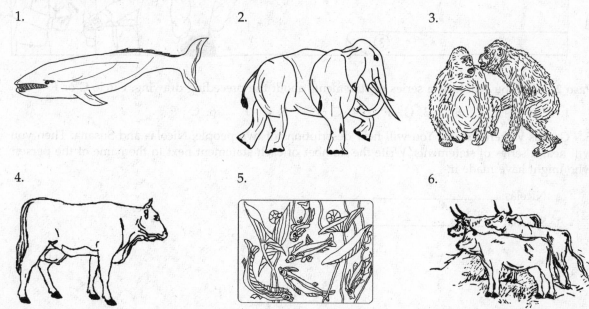

1.

2.

3.

4.

5.

6.

Paso 2. Preguntas. You will hear a series of questions. Each will be said twice. Answer using the animals depicted in the drawings in **Paso 1.**

1. ...   2. ...   3. ...   4. ...

C. Definiciones: Hablando de coches. You will hear a series of statements. Each will be said twice. Circle the letter of the word that is best defined by each.

1. a. la batería   b. la gasolina   c. la licencia

2. a. la licencia   b. el camino   c. el taller

3. a. el parabrisas   b. los frenos   c. el semáforo

4. a. la esquina   b. la carretera   c. la llanta

5. a. el accidente   b. el aceite   c. el taller

D. Un accidente

Paso 1. Identify the following items when you hear the corresponding number. Begin each sentence with **Es un… , Es una… ,** or **Son…**

Paso 2. Now you will hear a series of statements about the preceding drawing. Circle **C** or **F**.

1. C F   2. C F   3. C F   4. C F   5. C F   6. C F

E. Gustos y preferencias. You will hear descriptions of two people, Nicolás and Susana. Then you will hear a series of statements. Write the number of each statement next to the name of the person who might have made it.

Nicolás: _____

Susana: _____

■■■Los hispanos hablan: En tu opinión, ¿cuáles son las semejanzas y diferencias más grandes entre las ciudades hispánicas y las norteamericanas?

You will hear excerpts from several answers to this question. After you listen, pause and check the appropriate boxes to describe Hispanic and U.S. cities. The following words and phrases appear in the answers.

recorrer un gran trecho   *to travel a great distance*

no hace falta   no es necesario

las fuentes   *fountains*

como no sea   *unless it is (unless we are talking about)*

a la par de   al lado de

seguro   *safe*

	LAS CIUDADES HISPÁNICAS	LAS CIUDADES NORTEAMERICANAS
1. Son muy grandes.	☐	☐
2. Están contaminadas.	☐	☐
3. Tienen más vida.	☐	☐
4. Son menos seguras.	☐	☐
5. La gente vive en la ciudad misma (*proper*).	☐	☐
6. Las tiendas están en las vecindades.	☐	☐
7. Hay más árboles, vegetación y parques.	☐	☐

Now resume listening.

PRONUNCIACIÓN Y ORTOGRAFÍA   More Cognate Practice

A. Repeticiones. You were introduced to cognates in the **Ante todo** sections of *Puntos de partida*. As you know, English and Spanish cognates do not always share the same pronunciation or spelling. Listen to the following pairs of cognates, paying close attention to the differences in spelling and pronunciation.

chemical / químico   affirm / afirmar   national / nacional

Read the following cognates when you hear the corresponding number. Remember to repeat the correct pronunciation.

1. correcto
2. anual
3. teoría
4. alianza

5. físico
6. teléfono
7. patético
8. intención

B. Dictado. You will hear the following words. Each will be said twice. Listen carefully and write the missing letters. (Check your answers in the Appendix.)

1. _____os_____ato
2. a_____ención
3. a_____oníaco
4. _____eología

5. o_____osición
6. _____otogra_____ía
7. co_____e_____ión
8. ar_____itecta

GRAMÁTICA

42. Más descripciones • Past Participle Used as an Adjective

A. Gramática en acción: Algunos refranes y dichos en español. You will hear a series of statements. Write the number of each statement under the correct proverb or saying. First listen to the proverbs and sayings.

a. En boca *cerrada*
no entran moscas.

_____

b. Estar tan *aburrido*
como una ostra.

_____

c. Cuando está *abierto* el cajón,
el más *honrado* es ladrón.

_____

B. Descripción. Which picture is best described by the sentences you hear? You will hear each sentence twice.

VOCABULARIO ÚTIL: colgar   *to hang up*
                   enchufar   *to plug in*

1. a.

    b.

 Elsa

 Elsa

2. a.   b.

3. a.    b.

4. a.    b.

5. a.    b.

6. a.    b.

C. Definiciones. You will hear a series of definitions. Each will be said twice. Circle the answer that best matches each definition. ¡OJO! There may be more than one answer for some items.

1. a. el agua   b. el aire   c. la batería

2. a. Stephen King   b. Descartes   c. Dan Brown

3. a. la mano   b. los ojos   c. la ventana

4. a. el papel   b. el pie   c. la computadora

D. Consecuencias lógicas. You will hear a series of sentences that describe actions. Respond to each sentence, telling the probable outcome of the action.

> MODELO: (*you hear*) Escribí la composición. → (*you say*) Ahora la composición está escrita.

1. ... 2. ... 3. ... 4. ... 5. ...

43. ¿Qué has hecho? • Perfect Forms: Present Perfect Indicative and Present Perfect Subjunctive

A. Gramática en acción: Una llanta desinflada. You will hear a series of questions. Each will be said twice. No answers will be given. Circle the letter of the answer that is true for you!

1. a. Sí, le he cambiado una llanta desinflada a un carro.
    b. No, nunca le he cambiado una llanta desinflada a un carro.
2. a. Sí, le he revisado el aceite al coche.
    b. No, nunca se lo he revisado.
3. a. Sí, he tenido un accidente con el coche.
    b. No, no he tenido un accidente con el coche.
4. a. Sí, he excedido el límite de velocidad en la autopista.
    b. No, ¡nunca he hecho eso!

B. ¿Qué ha pasado ya? You will hear a series of sentences. Each will be said twice. Circle the letter of the subject of the verb in each sentence.

1. a. yo   b. ella

2. a. él   b. nosotros

3. a. nosotros   b. tú

4. a. nosotros   b. yo

5. a. ellos   b. él

C. ¿Qué hemos hecho hoy? Form new sentences, using the oral and written cues. Use the present perfect indicative of the verbs.

1. despertarse
2. hacer las camas
3. vestirse
4. desayunar
5. salir para la oficina
6. llevar el auto a la gasolinera

D. ¿Te puedo ayudar? Imagine that you have a lot to do before a dinner party, and your friend

Ernesto wants to know if he can help. You appreciate his offer, but you have already done the things he asks about. You will hear each of his questions twice. Answer them, according to the model.

> MODELO: (*you hear*) ¿Quieres que llame a los Sres. Moreno? →
> (*you say*) No, gracias, ya los he llamado.

1. ...   2. ...   3. ...   4. ...   5. ...

E. Un caso de contaminación ambiental. Imagine that a case of environmental pollution was discovered earlier this year in your community. Using the oral and written cues, form sentences that express what the residents have said about the incident. Follow the model.

> MODELO: (*you see*) ya estudiar el problema   (*you hear*) es probable →
> (*you say*) Es probable que ya hayan estudiado el problema.

1. todavía no avisar (*to notify*) a todos los habitantes de la ciudad
2. ya consultar con los expertos
3. encontrar la solución todavía
4. proteger los animales de la zona

UN POCO DE TODO | (Para entregar)

A. Descripciones. You will hear a series of descriptions. Each will be said twice. Write the number of each description next to the drawing described. ¡OJO! There is one extra drawing. First, pause and look at the drawings.

a. _____

b. _____

c. _____

d. _____

e. _____

B. Listening Passage: Los coches

Antes de escuchar. You will hear a passage about the types of cars driven in the Hispanic world. The following words appear in the passage.

la molestia	*bother*
la ayuda	*something helpful*
la clase media-baja	*lower middle class*

Listening Passage. Here is the passage. First, listen to it to get a general idea of the content. Then go back and listen again for specific information.

Después de escuchar. Read the following statements. Circle **C** or **F.** Correct the statements that are false, according to the passage.

1. C F Las personas que viven en los países hispanos no están acostumbradas a conducir.

   _____

2. C F Hay muchos autos japoneses y estadounidenses en España.

   _____

3. C F No se venden marcas europeas en Latinoamérica.

   _____

4. C F El precio de la gasolina es comparable en España y en los Estados Unidos.

   _____

5. C F En México, es posible encontrar marcas que ya no se fabrican en otras partes del mundo.

   _____

Now resume listening.

C. Y para terminar... Entrevista. You will hear a series of questions. Each will be said twice. Answer based on your own experience. Pause and write the answers.

1. _____

2. _____

3. _____

4. _____

5. _____

6. _____

7. _____

8. _____

VIDEOTECA — Minidramas*

Paso 1. En busca de un taller. In the following conversation, Elisa and José Miguel help out a motorist in trouble. Listen and read along with the speakers.

CONDUCTORA: Buenos días. Disculpe, señora. ¿Podría decirme a cuánto queda el pueblo más cercano?

ELISA: Bueno, hay un pueblo no muy lejos de aquí, como a unos diez minutos. Pero es muy pequeño. ¿Qué busca?

CONDUCTORA: Es el carro. Temo que tenga algo serio. Ha comenzado a hacer un ruido muy extraño, y quiero que lo revise un mecánico. ¿Sabe Ud. si hay un taller en el pueblo?

ELISA: Ay, lo dudo mucho. Pero hay otro pueblo más grande no muy lejos, y es muy posible que haya un taller allí. Siga todo derecho unos cinco kilómetros, y luego doble a la izquierda en la carretera para Quito. ¿Sabe? Se me ocurre algo. Nosotros vamos en esa dirección. La podemos acompañar. No me gusta que se quede sola en este camino con un carro que no arranca.

CONDUCTORA: Eso es muy amable de su parte, pero no se molesten.

JOSÉ MIGUEL: De veras, no es ninguna molestia. Necesitamos encontrar una gasolinera. Tenemos que llenar el tanque.

CONDUCTORA: Muchas gracias. Uds. me han ayudado muchísimo.

ELISA: No hay de qué. ¿Vamos?

Paso 2. Aplicación. Now you will participate in a conversation, partially printed in your manual, in which you play the role of a motorist (**conductor**) who needs help. You are now at the repair shop. Complete it using the written cues. You will need to conjugate the verbs. Here are the cues for your conversation. ¡OJO! The cues are not in order.

muchísimas gracias   ser el motor   ser un auto nuevo
revisarle las llantas y los frenos   tener algo serio   haber comenzado

CONDUCTOR: Temo que mi auto _____.¹ _____²
a hacer un ruido extraño.

MECÁNICO: Es posible que sea el motor.

CONDUCTOR: Dudo que _____³ ... _____⁴

MECÁNICO: En ese caso, le recomiendo que lo deje aquí para poder revisarlo con cuidado.

CONDUCTOR: Está bien. También quiero que _____⁵.

MECÁNICO: Por supuesto. Eso es parte de nuestro servicio normal. Puede venir a buscar su auto dentro de tres horas.

CONDUCTOR: _____⁶

*This **Minidramas** video clip is available on the DVD to accompany *Puntos de partida*, Eighth Edition.

PRUEBA CORTA

A. ¿Por qué no... ? The speaker will ask you why you don't do certain things. Answer her questions, following the model.

> MODELO: (*you hear*) ¿Por qué no resuelve Ud. ese problema? →
> (*you say*) Porque ya está resuelto.

1. ... 2. ... 3. ... 4. ... 5. ...

B. Cosas de todos los días: El medio ambiente. Practice talking about what has happened recently, using the written cues. When you hear the corresponding number, form sentences using the words provided in the order given, making any necessary changes or additions. ¡OJO! You will need to make changes to adjectives and add articles, if appropriate.

> MODELO: (*you see*) 1. gobierno / construir / mucha / carreteras / nuevo (*you hear*) uno →
> (*you say*) *El gobierno ha construido muchas carreteras nuevas.*

2. gobierno / tratar de / proteger / naturaleza
3. gobierno / no / resolver / problema / de / tránsito
4. alguno / compañías / desarrollar / energía / hidráulico
5. otro / compañías / descubrir / petróleo
6. público / no / conservar / energía

CAPÍTULO **15**

VOCABULARIO Preparación

A. Encuesta: Hablando de las relaciones sentimentales. You will hear a series of statements about personal relationships. Express your opinion by checking the appropriate box. No answers will be given. The answers you choose should be correct for you!

1. ☐ Sí   ☐ No   6. ☐ Sí   ☐ No

2. ☐ Sí   ☐ No   7. ☐ Sí   ☐ No

3. ☐ Sí   ☐ No   8. ☐ Sí   ☐ No

4. ☐ Sí   ☐ No   9. ☐ Sí   ☐ No

5. ☐ Sí   ☐ No   10. ☐ Sí   ☐ No

B. Definiciones. You will hear a series of definitions. Each will be said twice. Circle the letter of the word defined. ¡OJO! There is more than one answer for some items.

1. a. la amistad   b. el corazón   c. el amor

2. a. una separación   b. el divorcio   c. una visita al consejero matrimonial

3. a. la luna de miel   b. la cita   c. la pareja

4. a. el noviazgo   b. la boda   c. la cita

5. a. la dueña   b. la consejera   c. la novia

C. Asociaciones. You will hear a series of phrases. Each will be said twice. Circle the letter of the word that you associate with each.

1. a. la infancia   b. la niñez   c. la adolescencia

2. a. la vejez   b. la juventud   c. el nacimiento

3. a. la madurez   b. la adolescencia   c. la infancia

4. a. la infancia   b. la vejez   c. la juventud

■■■Los hispanos hablan: Las relaciones sociales

As you might expect, social relations differ from country to country. You will hear Eduardo's impressions of the differences in social relations between the United States and his native country, Uruguay. The passage has been divided into two parts. Remember to concentrate on the vocabulary you know. Don't be distracted by unfamiliar vocabulary.

Paso 1. Before you listen to the passage, pause and indicate if the following statements are true for you. There are no right or wrong answers.

1. ☐ Sí   ☐ No   Me gusta que mis amigos vengan a visitarme sin avisar (*without letting me know ahead of time*).

2. ☐ Sí   ☐ No   Por lo general, mi vida social es espontánea; es decir, generalmente, no planeo todas mis actividades.

3. ☐ Sí   ☐ No   Participo en actividades sociales en las cuales (*in which*) hay personas de varias generaciones (niños, jóvenes, personas de mi edad, personas mayores o viejas).

4. ☐ Sí   ☐ No   Para mí, la vida privada (*privacy*) es algo importante.

5. ☐ Sí   ☐ No   Todavía vivo con mi familia.

Now resume listening.

La vida social: Parte 1. The following words appear in the first part of the passage.

extrañan	*they miss*
se dedica	*spend a lot of time on* (*something*)
sin avisar	*without letting one know ahead of time*
mal visto	*not looked upon favorably*

La vida social: Parte 2. The following words appear in the second part of the passage.

la vida privada	*privacy*
insólito	*unusual*

Paso 2. Now, pause and write a brief paragraph that summarizes how Eduardo feels about social relations in the United States. It may help to look back at the statements you read before listening to the passage. (Compare your paragraph to the text in the Appendix.)

Eduardo piensa que... _____

_____

_____

_____

_____

_____

_____

_____

Now resume listening.

PRONUNCIACIÓN Y ORTOGRAFÍA

More Cognate Practice

A. Amigos falsos. Unlike true cognates, false cognates do not have the same meaning in English as they do in Spanish. Repeat the following words, some of which you have already seen and used actively, paying close attention to their pronunciation and true meaning in Spanish.

> la carta (*letter*)
> dime (*tell me*)
> emocionante (*thrilling*)
> asistir (*to attend*)
> el pan (*bread*)
> el éxito (*success*)
> sin (*without*)
> el pie (*foot*)
> actual (*current, present-day*)
> actualmente (*nowadays*)
> embarazada (*pregnant*)
> el pariente (*relative*)
> dice (*he/she says*)
> la red (*net*)

B. Un satélite español. You will hear the following paragraphs from an article in a Spanish newspaper. Pay close attention to the pronunciation of the indicated cognates. Then you will practice reading the paragraphs.

El *ministro* de *Transportes* y *Comunicaciones*, Abel Caballero, ha *declarado* que el Gobierno está dando los primeros pasos para la *construcción* de un *satélite* español de *telecomunicaciones* que, de tomarse la *decisión final, comenzará* a ser *operativo* el año que viene.

Muchos de los *componentes* del *satélite* tendrían que ser *importados*, pero al menos el treinta y seis por ciento los podría construir la *industria* española.

Now, pause and read the paragraphs. You may also wish to go back and read along with the speaker.

Now resume listening.

44. ¿Hay alguien que... ? ¿Hay un lugar donde... ? • The Subjunctive (Part 6): The Subjunctive After Nonexistent and Indefinite Antecedents

A. Gramática en acción: Un buen lunes. You will hear a paragraph about Mafalda's father and what other children need in a father. As you listen, circle the verb form that you hear. First, pause and read the following cartoon.

© Joaquín Salvador Lavado (QUINO) *Toda Mafalda*—Ediciones de La Flor, 1993

°eres (*Arg.*)

Now resume listening.

Mafalda tiene un padre que la (quiere / quiera),[1] la (proteja / protege)[2] y que (comparta / comparte)[3] (*shares*) su tiempo con ella. Por eso, Mafalda ve a su padre como un hombre que ahora es más guapo que cuando era joven. Todos los niños necesitan padres que los (quieren / quieran),[4] los (cuiden / cuidan)[5] y que (tienen / tengan)[6] tiempo para estar con ellos.

B. En busca de una nueva casa. Form new sentences, using the oral cues.

1. (*you see and hear*) ¿Qué tipo de casa buscan Uds.? (*you hear*) estar en el campo →
   (*you say*) Buscamos una casa que esté en el campo.

   a. ... b. ... c. ...

2. (*you see and hear*) ¿Y cómo quieren Uds. que sean los vecinos? (*you hear*) jugar a las cartas →
   (*you say*) Queremos vecinos que jueguen a las cartas.

   a. ... b. ... c. ...

C. Escenas de la vida. You will hear a series of statements. Each will be said twice. Respond to each statement, using the written cues.

> MODELO: (*you hear*) Necesitamos un secretario que hable español.
> (*you see*) Pues, yo conozco... →
> (*you say*) Pues, yo conozco a un secretario que habla español.

1. Yo te puedo recomendar...
2. Lo siento, pero no hay nadie aquí...
3. Pues yo busco...
4. Pues yo también quiero...
5. Ellos van a ofrecerte un puesto...

D. ¿Qué quieren estas personas? You will hear what these people already have. Say what they want, using the written cues. If you prefer, pause and write the answers.

MODELO: (*you see*) es viejo / ser nuevo →
 (*you hear*) Arturo tiene un auto que es viejo.
 (*you say*) Quiere un auto que sea nuevo.

1. no tiene vista / tener vista

_____

_____

2. es perezoso / ser trabajador

_____

_____

3. es muy grande / ser pequeño

_____

_____

4. hacen mucho ruido / no hacer tanto ruido

_____

_____

45. Lo hago para que tú... • The Subjunctive (Part 7): The Subjunctive After Conjunctions of Contingency and Purpose

A. Gramática en acción: Maneras de amar

Paso 1. Dictado. You will hear three statements about the following drawings. Listen carefully and write the missing words. (Check your answers in the Appendix.) (The short lines under the drawings are for **Paso 2.**)

a.

_____

b.

_____

c.

_____

1. Quiero _____ contigo para que _____ siempre juntos y no

    _____ más con Raúl.

2. _____ bien: no vas a salir _____ de que _____

    la tarea. ¿Me entiendes?

3. Aquí tienes la tarjeta de crédito, pero _____ sólo en _____ de

    que _____ una emergencia, ¿eh?

Paso 2. ¿Quién lo dijo? Now, pause and write the number of each statement under the corresponding drawing.

Now resume listening.

B. Antes del viaje. You will hear a dialogue between Francisco and Araceli about their upcoming trip. Then you will hear a series of statements. Circle **C, F,** or **ND** (**No lo dice**).

1. C F ND

2. C F ND

3. C F ND

4. C F ND

5. C F ND

C. Un viaje. You will hear the following pairs of sentences. Then you will hear a conjunction. Join each pair of sentences, using the conjunction and making any necessary changes.

> MODELO: (*you see and hear*) Hacemos el viaje. No cuesta mucho. (*you hear*) con tal que →
> (*you say*) Hacemos el viaje con tal que no cueste mucho.

1. Tenemos que salir. Empieza a llover.
2. No queremos ir. Hace sol.
3. Pon las maletas en el coche. Podemos salir pronto.
4. Trae el mapa. Nos perdemos.

D. ¿Quién lo dijo? When you hear the number, read aloud each of the following statements, giving the present subjunctive form of the verb in parentheses. You will hear the correct answer. Then you will hear the names of two different people. Circle the letter of the person who might have made each statement.

1. a b No les doy los paquetes a los clientes antes de que me (*pagar*).
2. a b Voy a revisar las llantas en caso de que (*necesitar*) aire.
3. a b No compro esa computadora a menos que (*ser*) fácil de manejar.
4. a b Voy a tomarle la temperatura al paciente antes de que lo (*ver*) la doctora.

UN POCO DE TODO | (Para entregar)

A. Identificaciones. You will hear six sentences. Each will be said twice. Write the number of each sentence next to the drawing that is described. ¡OJO! There are two extra drawings. First, pause and look at the drawings.

a. _____

b. _____

c. _____

d. _____

e. _____

f. _____

g. _____

h. _____

B. *Listening Passage:* **Semejanzas y diferencias**

Antes de escuchar. You will hear a conversation, already in progress, between two students: one is from Spain and the other is from the United States. They are talking about the similarities and differences between people of their age group in the United States and Spain. Notice that the student from Spain uses the **vosotros** forms of verbs, pronouns, and possessive adjectives instead of the **Uds.** forms. Although the **vosotros** forms are not frequently used in *Puntos de partida*, you should be able to recognize them.

Listening Passage. The following words and phrases appear in the conversation.

nos independizamos	*we become independent*
me di cuenta que	*I realized*
no se ve tan mal	*it is not looked down upon (considered odd, viewed as bad)*
dura	*lasts*
los préstamos	*loans*
las becas	*scholarships, grants*
los ingresos	*earnings, assets*
estatales	*state run (adj.)*

Después de escuchar. Indicate the country to which the following sentences refer, based on the conversation that you just heard.

	ESPAÑA	LOS ESTADOS UNIDOS
1. La mayoría de las universidades son estatales.	☐	☐
2. Es normal obtener un préstamo para asistir a la universidad.	☐	☐
3. Es normal que una persona mayor de 18 años viva con sus padres.	☐	☐
4. Se ve mal que los hijos vivan con la familia después de cumplir los dieciocho años.	☐	☐
5. La universidad dura cinco años, generalmente.	☐	☐
6. A los jóvenes les gusta la música *rock* y llevar *jeans*.	☐	☐

Now resume listening.

C. Y para terminar... Entrevista. You will hear a series of questions. Each will be said twice. Answer based on your own experience. Pause and write the answers. Write out all numbers as words.

1. _____

2. _____

3. _____

4. _____

5. _____

6. _____

VIDEOTECA   Minidramas*

Paso 1. Una invitación. In this conversation, Lola and her friend Eva make plans for the weekend. Listen and read along with the speakers.

LOLA: ¡Por fin es viernes! Qué semana más larga, ¿eh?

EVA: ¿Qué vais a hacer este fin de semana?

LOLA: Pues, nos vamos a pasar el día con mi hermano en Cádiz. Es el cumpleaños de mi sobrino. Y el domingo no tenemos planes. Y vosotros, ¿qué hacéis?

EVA: El domingo vamos a una boda aquí en Sevilla. Se casa una prima mía. ¿Tenéis planes para esta noche?

LOLA: Creo que no, a menos que Manolo haya hecho planes.

EVA: ¿Y por qué no salimos todos juntos? ¡Hace tanto tiempo que no lo hacemos!

LOLA: Por mí, encantada. Podemos ir a cenar o al cine. Hay dos o tres películas interesantes que a Manolo y a mí nos gustaría ver. También podemos llevar a las niñas. ¡Carolina y Marta ya son como hermanas! Se lo voy a preguntar a Manolo y te llamo después.

EVA: Muy bien. Yo también hablo con Jesús. Hablamos luego y entonces decidimos qué hacer, ¿vale?

LOLA: Estupendo.

---

*This **Minidramas** video clip is available on the DVD to accompany *Puntos de partida*, Eighth Edition.

Paso 2. Aplicación. Now you will participate in a similar conversation, partially printed in your manual, in which you play the role of **Ud.** Complete it using the written cues. You will need to conjugate the verbs. Here are the cues for your conversation. ¡OJO! Use the cues in the order given.

> estar libre / esta tarde
>
> venir conmigo / tomar un café

UD.: ¡Hola, Yolanda! ¡Hace tiempo que no te veo! ¿_____?[1]

YOLANDA: ¡Qué coincidencia! Te iba a llamar anoche. Resulta que no tengo que trabajar esta tarde.

UD.: ¡Magnífico! ¿Quieres _____?[2]

YOLANDA: Pues, ¡claro! Tengo un montón (*lot*) que contarte…

PRUEBA CORTA

A. En busca de los amigos perfectos. Practice talking about ideal friends. When you hear the corresponding number, form sentences using the written cues. Begin each sentence with **Quiero…** Make any necessary changes or additions.

> MODELO: (*you see*) 1. amigo / ser / simpático → (*you hear*) uno
> (*you say*) Quiero *un* amigo *que sea simpático.*

2. amiga / ser / amable
3. amigos / ser / flexible
4. amigas / vivir / cerca de mí
5. amigo / tener / coche
6. amiga / saber / mucho de computadoras

B. Cosas de todos los días: La boda de Mireya y Alonso. Practice talking about Mireya and Alonso's upcoming wedding, using the written cues. When you hear the corresponding number, form sentences using the words provided in the order given, making any necessary changes or additions. ¡OJO! You will need to make changes to adjectives and add articles, if appropriate.

> MODELO: (*you see*) 1. padre de Mireya / pensar / que / (ellos) no deber / casarse /
> a menos que / (ellos) / llevarse bien (*you hear*) uno →
> (*you say*) *El* padre de Mireya *piensa* que no *deben casarse* a menos que *se lleven* bien.

2. padres de Alonso / pensar / que / (ellos) deber / casarse / con tal que / (ellos) estar / enamorado
3. Mireya / pensar / confirmar / fecha / antes de que / su / padres / mandar / invitaciones
4. padres de Mireya / ir / alquilar / sala / grande / en caso de que / venir / mucho / invitados
5. (ellos) pensar / regalarles / dinero / para que / novios / empezar / ahorrar (*to save*)
6. Mireya y Alonso / ir / pasar / luna de miel / en Cancún / con tal que / poder / encontrar / hotel / barato

CAPÍTULO 16

Preparación

A. ¿A quién necesitan en estas situaciones? You will hear a series of situations. Each will be said twice. Circle the letter of the person or professional who would best be able to help.

1. a. un arquitecto   b. un analista de sistemas
2. a. una dentista   b. una enfermera
3. a. una consejera matrimonial b. un policía
4. a. una fotógrafa   b. un bibliotecario
5. a. un plomero   b. una electricista

B. ¿Quiénes son? Using the list of professions below, identify these people after you hear the corresponding number. Begin each sentence with **Es un...** or **Es una...** . First, listen to the list of professions.

obrero/a   cocinero/a
peluquero/a   fotógrafo/a
periodista   plomero/a
veterinario/a   hombre o mujer de negocios

1.   2.   3.   4.   5.   6.   7.   8.

C. En busca de un puesto

Paso 1. Imagine that you are looking for a new job in a large corporation. Tell how you will go about getting the job, using phrases from the following list. First, listen to the list, then pause and put the remaining items in order, from 3 to 6. (Check your answers in the Appendix before you begin **Paso 2.**)

_____ contestar preguntas sobre mi experiencia

_____ aceptar el puesto y renunciar a mi puesto actual

___2___ pedir una solicitud de empleo

_____ ir a la entrevista

_____ llenar la solicitud

___1___ llamar la oficina de empleos

Now resume listening.

Paso 2. Now tell what you will do to look for a job when you hear the numbers. Follow the model.

> MODELO: (*you hear*) uno   (*you see*) llamar la oficina de empleos →
> (*you say*) Llamo la oficina de empleos.

D. Descripción. You will hear a series of questions. Each will be said twice. Answer based on the drawing. If you prefer, pause and write the answers.

1. _____

2. _____

3. _____

4. _____

5. _____

■■■Los hispanos hablan: ¿Cuáles son las profesiones de más prestigio (*prestige*) en su país? ¿Qué profesión es menos apreciada?

You will hear two answers to these questions. Then, after each answer, you will hear a series of statements about the answer. Circle **C** or **F**. The following words appear in the answers.

el agente de bolsa	*stockbroker*
la remuneración	el pago (el sueldo)
sea cual sea su profesión	no importa la profesión que tenga
la enseñanza	*teaching*
remuneradas	pagadas

Habla Tomás, un arquitecto español

   1. C F   2. C F   3. C F

Habla Francisco, un científico español

   1. C F   2. C F   3. C F

PRONUNCIACIÓN Y ORTOGRAFÍA — More on Stress and the Written Accent

A. El acento escrito y los verbos. You have learned that the written accent is an important factor in the spelling of some verbs. You know that in the case of the preterite, for example, a missing accent can change the meaning of the verb. Listen to the following pairs of words.

habló	(*he, she, or you spoke*)	/ hablo	(*I am speaking or I speak*)
hablé	(*I spoke*)	/ hable	(*that he, she, you, or I may speak—present subjunctive; speak* [formal command])

When you hear the corresponding number, read the following pairs of words. Then repeat the correct pronunciation, imitating the speaker.

1. tomo / tomó
2. ahorro / ahorró
3. pague / pagué

B. El acento escrito. The written accent also is important in maintaining the original stress of a word to which syllables have been added. In the word **jóvenes,** for example, the written accent maintains the stress of the singular word **joven,** even though another syllable has been added. Sometimes, the reverse will be true. A word that has a written accent will lose the accent when a syllable is added. Compare **inglés** and **ingleses.** This happens because the new word receives the stress naturally; that is, it follows the rules of stress.

When you hear the corresponding number, read the following groups of words. Then repeat the correct pronunciation, imitating the speaker.

1. dígame / dígamelo
2. póngase / póngaselo
3. escriba / escríbanos
4. depositen / depósitenlos
5. almacén / almacenes
6. nación / naciones

C. Dictado. You will hear the following words. Each will be said twice. Write in an accent mark, if necessary. (Check your answers in the Appendix.)

1. cobro
2. cobro
3. toque
4. toque
5. describe
6. describemela
7. levantate
8. levanta
9. franceses
10. frances

D. El acento diacrítico. You have probably noticed that when a pair of words is written the same but has different meanings, one of the words is accented. This accent is called a *diacritical* accent.

Listen to and repeat the following words, paying close attention to the meaning of each.

1. mi (*my*) / mí (*me*)
2. tu (*your*) / tú (*you*)
3. el (*the*) / él (*he*)
4. si (*if*) / sí (*yes*)
5. se (*oneself*) / sé (*I know; be* [informal command])
6. de (*of, from*) / dé (*give* [formal command]; *give* [present subjunctive])
7. te (*you, yourself*) / té (*tea*)
8. solo (*alone, sole* [adjective]) / sólo (*only* [adverb])
9. que (*that, which*) / ¿qué? (*what?*)

E. Dictado. Listen to the following sentences. Determine by context whether or not the meaning of the italicized words requires a written accent. If so, write it in. Each sentence will be said twice. (Check your answers in the Appendix.)

1. Creo *que* ese regalo es para *mi*.
2. Aquí *esta tu te*. ¿*Que* más quieres?
3. *El* dijo *que te* iba a llamar a las ocho.
4. *Si, mi* amigo *se* llama Antonio.

GRAMÁTICA

46. Talking About the Future • Future Verb Forms

A. Gramática en acción: ¿Qué será, será?: Encuesta. You will hear a series of questions about your future. No answers will be given. The answers you choose should be correct for you!

	SÍ	NO			SÍ	NO
1.	☐	☐		4.	☐	☐
2.	☐	☐		5.	☐	☐
3.	☐	☐		6.	☐	☐

B. Un futuro perfecto

Paso 1. You will hear a brief paragraph in which Angélica talks about her future. Then you will hear a series of statements. Circle **C, F,** or **ND.**

1. C F ND

2. C F ND

3. C F ND

4. C F ND

5. C F ND

Paso 2. Now pause and complete the following statements according to your own preferences. No answers will be given.

1. Cuando yo me gradúe, _____

2. Trabajaré para _____

3. Viviré en _____

4. Mi casa será _____

5. Tendré un auto _____

6. Pasaré mis vacaciones en _____

7. Mi vida será _____

Now resume listening.

C. El viernes por la tarde.
Using the oral and written cues, tell what the following people will do with their paychecks.

1. Bernardo
2. Adela y yo
3. tú... ¿verdad?
4. yo

D. El cumpleaños de Jaime.
Jaime's birthday is next week. Answer the questions about his birthday, using the written cues. Each question will be said twice.

MODELO: (*you hear*) ¿Cuántos años va a cumplir Jaime? (*you see*) dieciocho →
(*you say*) Cumplirá dieciocho años.

1. sus amigos y sus parientes
2. un iPod
3. un pastel de chocolate
4. discos compactos
5. ¡Feliz cumpleaños!

47. Expressing Future or Pending Actions • The Subjunctive (Part 8): Subjunctive and Indicative After Conjunctions of Time

A. Gramática en acción: Planes para el futuro

Paso 1. ¿Quién lo dijo? You will hear three statements about the following drawings. Write the number of each statement under the correct drawing.

a.

b.

c.

_____   _____   _____

Paso 2. ¿Cierto o falso? You will hear a series of statements about the preceding drawings and accompanying statements. Circle **C** or **F**. You may want to listen again to the statements from **Paso 1** before beginning **Paso 2**.

1. C F   4. C F
2. C F   5. C F
3. C F

B. Escenas de la vida cotidiana. You will hear the following pairs of sentences. Combine them to form one complete sentence, using the oral cues.

> MODELO: (*you see and hear*) Voy a decidirlo. Hablo con él. (*you hear*) después de que →
> (*you say*) Voy a decidirlo después de que hable con él.

1. Amalia va a viajar. Consigue un poco de dinero.
2. No estaré contenta. Recibo un aumento.
3. Podrán ahorrar más. Sus hijos terminan sus estudios.
4. Tito, devuélveme el dinero. Se te olvida.

C. Asuntos económicos. You will hear a series of incomplete sentences. Circle the letter of the correct ending for each, then repeat the completed sentence. ¡OJO! In this exercise, you will be choosing between the present subjunctive and the present indicative.

> MODELO: (*you hear*) Voy a depositar mi cheque cuando... a. lo reciba b. lo recibo →
> (*you say*) a. Voy a depositar mi cheque cuando lo reciba.

1. a. las reciba
   b. las recibo
2. a. tenga más dinero
   b. tengo más dinero
3. a. consiga otro puesto
   b. consigo otro puesto
4. a. lo firme (*sign*)
   b. lo firmo

UN POCO DE TODO (Para entregar)

A. ¿Qué cree Ud. que van a hacer estas personas? You will hear three situations. Each will be said twice. Choose the most logical solution for each and repeat it.

1. a. Teresa comprará un coche barato y económico.
   b. Comprará un coche de lujo (*luxury*).
   c. No comprará ningún coche.
2. a. Basilio tendrá que conseguir otro trabajo para pagar el nuevo alquiler.
   b. Robará un banco.
   c. Compartirá (*He will share*) su apartamento con cuatro amigos.
3. a. Luisa empezará a poner el dinero que gasta en diversiones en su cuenta de ahorros.
   b. Ella comprará el regalo la próxima semana.
   c. Insistirá en que su jefe le dé un aumento de sueldo inmediatamente.

B. Listening Passage: El sistema universitario hispánico

Antes de escuchar. You will hear a passage about the differences between the university system in most of the Hispanic world and that of the United States. The following words appear in the passage.

la etapa	*stage*	una vez que	*once*
suele durar	*usually lasts*	el requisito	*requirement*
se matricula	*enrolls*	la profundidad	*depth*
por lo tanto	*therefore*		

Listening Passage. Here is the passage. First, listen to it to get a general idea of the content. Then go back and listen again for specific information.

Después de escuchar. Indicate whether the following statements refer to the Hispanic world or to the United States, according to the information in the passage.

	EL MUNDO HISPÁNICO	LOS ESTADOS UNIDOS
1. La mayoría de las carreras duran menos de cinco años.	☐	☐
2. Al entrar (*Upon entering*) en la universidad, un estudiante se matricula directamente en el área de su especialización.	☐	☐
	☐	☐
3. El estudiante tiene pocas opciones una vez que empieza sus estudios.	☐	☐
4. Hay requisitos «generales» como ciencias naturales, ciencias sociales o humanidades.	☐	☐
5. El currículum es bastante estricto.	☐	☐
6. Los estudios que se hacen para una licenciatura son bastante profundos y variados.	☐	☐
7. Por lo general, la especialización no se «declara» el primer año de estudios universitarios.	☐	☐

Now resume listening.

C. En el periódico: Empleos. The following ads for jobs appeared in a Mexican newspaper. Choose the ad you are most interested in, based on the profession, and scan it. Then, after you hear each question, answer it based on the ad. If the information requested is not in the ad, write **No lo dice.** First, pause and look at the ads. Pause to write the answers.

1. _____

2. _____

3. _____

4. _____

5. _____

IMPORTANTE EMPRESA FARMACEUTICA, REQUIERE

QUIMICO ANALISTA

(QBP, QSB, QFI o equivalente)

REQUISITOS:
- Ambos sexos
- Edad de 25 a 45 años
- Experiencia un año en el área de microbiología
- Antecedentes de estabilidad de trabajos anteriores

OFRECEMOS:
- ★ Sueldo y prestaciones muy atractivas

Interesados presentarse o concertar cita con el **Lic. FERNANDO MARTINEZ en AVENIDA 1o. DE MAYO No. 130. Naucalpan de Juárez, Edo. de México. Tel. 576-00-44.**

IMPORTANTE EMPRESA TEXTIL, SOLICITA:

SECRETARIAS

Requisitos: Experiencia de 1 a 3 años, excelente presentación

AUXILIAR DE CONTABILIDAD

Requisitos: Escolaridad mínima 5o. semestre de la carrera de C.P., con o sin experiencia

Ofrecemos: Sueldo según aptitudes, prestaciones superiores a las de la ley, magnífico ambiente de trabajo

Interesados presentarse en: **AV. VIA MORELOS No. 68, XALOSTOC, EDO. DE MEXICO. Tel. 569-29-00.**

At'n. Departamento de Personal.

SOLICITA:

ANALISTA DE SISTEMAS

REQUISITOS:
- Dos años de experiencia mínima en VSE/SP o VM, DOS, JCL, VSAM, CICS, COBOL deseable
- Conocimientos de SQL, CSP

PROGRAMADOR

- Dos años de experiencia mínima en alguno de los siguientes lenguajes: COBOL (preferentemente), RPG, EDL, deseable
- Conocimientos de: DBASE III, LOTUS, DISPLAY-WRITE

Todos los candidatos deberán tener estudios profesionales (preferentemente), de 25 a 35 años de edad y excelente presentación.

Por nuestra parte ofrecemos:
- ★ Una compensación económica bastante competitiva, un paquete de prestaciones muy superiores a las de ley y amplias posibilidades de desarrollo

Interesados concertar cita al 541-30-60 y 541-61-00. Atención licenciado HERNANDEZ.

IMPORTANTE EMPRESA SOLICITA

EJECUTIVA DE VENTAS

Para Agencias de Viajes

REQUISITOS:
- Egresada de la carrera en Administración de Empresas Turísticas
- Excelente presentación
- Edad de 20 a 30 años
- Disponibilidad inmediata

OFRECEMOS:
- Sueldo según aptitudes
- Prestaciones de ley
- Agradable ambiente de trabajo

Interesados presentarse de lunes a viernes en horas hábiles en PLATEROS 31, San José Insurgentes.

IMPORTANTE GRUPO INDUSTRIAL EN NAUCALPAN, SOLICITA:

CONTRALOR CORPORATIVO

REQUISITOS:

- Contador Público ● Mayor de 35 años ● Sexo masculino ● Experiencia 5 años en manejo de empresas Holding, Planeación Fiscal, Consolidación, Trato con Consultores y Sistemas de Información ● Casado ● Sin problemas de horario.

Interesados, enviar curriculum vitae, mencionando pretensiones, al APARTADO POSTAL 150-A, Centro Cívico, C.P. 53100, Ciudad Satélite, Estado de México. U R G E N T E

Now resume listening.

D. Y para terminar... Entrevista. You will hear a series of questions. Each will be said twice. Answer based on your own experience. Pause and write the answers. Note that in number six, you will need to write a longer answer.

1. _____
2. _____
3. _____
4. _____
5. _____
6. _____
   _____
   _____
   _____
   _____

VIDEOTECA　Minidramas*

Paso 1. Lupe solicita un puesto. In the following conversation, Lupe is being interviewed for a position as a receptionist in a bank. Read the conversation along with the speakers.

SRA. IBÁÑEZ: He hablado con varios aspirantes para el puesto de recepcionista, pero Ud. tiene el currículum más interesante. Veo que ha trabajado como recepcionista en la oficina de un abogado. ¿Por qué renunció a ese trabajo?

LUPE: Bueno, soy estudiante en la universidad. Me gustaba mucho el trabajo en la oficina del abogado, pero querían que trabajara la jornada completa. Desafortunadamente, no me era posible.

SRA. IBÁÑEZ: Y cuando trabajaba para el abogado, ¿cuáles eran sus responsabilidades?

LUPE: Contestaba el teléfono, hacía las citas con los clientes, organizaba el archivo... también le llevaba sus cuentas y pagaba los gastos básicos de la oficina. Eran las típicas responsabilidades de una recepcionista.

SRA. IBÁÑEZ: Ajá, entiendo. Srta. Carrasco, buscamos una persona que sea amable, que aprenda rápidamente, que sepa escribir a máquina y utilizar una computadora y que tenga paciencia con los clientes. Parece que Ud. cumple con estos requisitos. ¿Podrá asistir a un entrenamiento de seis horas la semana que viene?

LUPE: Sí, Sra. Ibáñez.

SRA. IBÁÑEZ: ¿Y podrá trabajar de vez en cuando en las otras sucursales del banco?

LUPE: ¡Claro que sí! No hay problema.

SRA. IBÁÑEZ: Muy bien.

This **Minidramas** video clip is available on the DVD to accompany *Puntos de partida*, Eighth Edition.

Paso 2. Aplicación. Now you will participate in a similar conversation, partially printed in your manual, in which you play the role of **Ud.** and answer questions about your imaginary job. Complete it using the written cues. Here are the cues for your conversation. ¡OJO! The cues are not in order.

es muy amable   ya encontraste trabajo

fantástico   tres semanas

AMIGA: ¡Hola! Hace tiempo que no te veo. ¿Qué tal te va en tu nuevo trabajo?

UD.: ¡_____!¹ Es un puesto estupendo.

AMIGA: Y tu jefa, ¿cómo es?

UD.: _____.² Nos llevamos muy bien.

AMIGA: Espero que te den vacaciones este año.

UD.: Sí, sí… Fíjate que me dan _____.³ Y tú,

¿_____?⁴

AMIGA: ¡Qué va! Todavía ando buscando…

PRUEBA CORTA

A. ¿Cuándo? You will hear a series of statements about what your friends plan to do. Ask them when they plan to do these things, using the future tense. Follow the model.

MODELO: (*you hear*) Voy a pagar mis cuentas → (*you say*) ¿Cuándo *las pagarás*?
(*you hear*) Las pagaré la próxima semana.

1. …   2. …   3. …   4. …   5. …

B. Cosas de todos los días: Empleos diversos. Practice talking about what people in various jobs do or will do, using the written cues. When you hear the corresponding number, form sentences using the words provided in the order given, making any necessary changes or additions. Use the indicative or the subjunctive, as appropriate. ¡OJO! You will need to make changes to adjectives and add articles and prepositions, if appropriate.

MODELO: (*you see*) 1. técnica / arreglar (*future*) / computadoras / cuando / llegar / oficina
(*you hear*) uno →
(*you see*) La técnica *arreglará las* computadoras cuando *llegue a la* oficina.

2. periodista (*m.*) / entrevistar (*future*) / empleados / antes de que / publicarse / artículo
3. vendedora / siempre / depositar (*present*) / cheques / después de que / recibirlos
4. ingeniera / viajar (*future*) / Acapulco / cuando / jubilarse
5. veterinario / mudarse (*future*) / tan pronto como / encontrar / nuevo / oficina
6. traductora / siempre / hacer (*present*) / traducción / en cuanto / leer / documentos
7. obreros / no / trabajar (*future*) / hasta que / recibir / bueno / aumento de sueldo

Nombre _____ Fecha _____ Clase _____

VOCABULARIO Preparación

A. Encuesta: ¿Con qué frecuencia... ? You will hear a series of statements about different ways of learning about what goes on in the world. For each statement, check the appropriate answer. No answers will be given. The answers you choose should be correct for you!

	TODOS LOS DÍAS	DE VEZ EN CUANDO	CASI NUNCA
1.	☐	☐	☐
2.	☐	☐	☐
3.	☐	☐	☐
4.	☐	☐	☐
5.	☐	☐	☐
6.	☐	☐	☐
7.	☐	☐	☐
8.	☐	☐	☐

B. El noticiero del Canal 10. You will hear a brief "newsbreak" from a television station. Then you will hear a series of statements about the newscast. Circle **C, F,** or **ND.**

1. C F ND   3. C F ND   5. C F ND

2. C F ND   4. C F ND

C. Definiciones. You will hear a series of statements. Each will be said twice. Place the number of the statement next to the word that is best defined by each. First, listen to the list of words.

_____ una guerra   _____ la testigo

_____ la prensa   _____ el reportero

_____ un dictador   _____ la huelga

_____ los terroristas   _____ el noticiero

D. Opiniones. You will hear a series of statements. Each will be said twice. React to each statement, using expressions chosen from the list. Be sure to express your own opinion. You will hear a possible answer. If you prefer, pause and write the answers.

Dudo que...

Es cierto que...

Es verdad que...

No es cierto que...

1. _____

2. _____

3. _____

4. _____

5. _____

6. _____

■■■Los hispanos hablan: Más sobre las ciudades hispánicas

When asked about some of the differences between U.S. cities and the Hispanic city in which she lives, Cecilia mentioned that some of the laws were different. As you listen to her answer, write down the effect she thinks each law or situation has on the population. (Check your answers in the Appendix.)

LEY O SITUACIÓN   RESULTADO

1. Un horario para volver a casa
   _____
   _____

2. Una edad permitida para tomar bebidas
   alcohólicas
   _____
   _____

3. Los chicos mayores de dieciocho años
   están en la universidad
   _____
   _____

PRONUNCIACIÓN Y ORTOGRAFÍA   Intonation, Punctuation, and Rhythm (Review of Linking)

A. La entonación. As you have probably noticed throughout the audio program and from listening to your instructor in class, intonation plays an important role in Spanish. The meaning of a sentence can change according to its intonation and punctuation. Listen to the following sentences. The arrows indicate a falling or rising intonation.

Los reporteros están aquí. (*statement*)

¿Los reporteros están aquí? (*question*)

¡Los reporteros están aquí! (*exclamation*)

B. Repeticiones. Repeat the following sentences, paying particular attention to punctuation, intonation, and rhythm.

1. ¿Ya destruyeron el edificio?

2. ¡Es imposible que construyan eso en la ciudad!

3. ¿Ya hablaste con la consejera?

4. Prepararon la cena, ¿verdad? Espero que ya esté lista (*ready*) porque ¡tengo mucha hambre!

5. Ojalá que no perdamos el vuelo... Tenemos que estar en Los Ángeles antes de las ocho de

    la noche.

C. La entonación. When you hear the corresponding number, read the following sentences. Then repeat them, imitating the speaker. Write in arrows to indicate rising or falling intonation. (Check your answers in the Appendix.)

1. Enero es el primer mes del año.

2. ¡No entiendo lo que me estás diciendo!

3. ¿Trabajaba en una tienda?

4. No olvides el diccionario la próxima vez, ¿eh?

5. Nació el catorce de abril de mil novecientos sesenta y uno.

6. ¿Adónde crees que vas a ir a estas horas de la noche?

D. Dictado. You will hear the following sentences. Each will be said twice. Listen carefully for intonation. Repeat what you hear, then punctuate each sentence. (Check your answers in the Appendix.)

1. Cuál es tu profesión   Te pagan bien

2. Tú no la conoces verdad

3. Prefiere Ud. que le sirva la comida en el patio

4. Qué ejercicio más fácil

5. No sé dónde viven pero sí sé su número de teléfono

GRAMÁTICA

48. ¡No queríamos que fuera así! • The Subjunctive (Part 9): The Past Subjunctive

A. Gramática en acción: Las últimas elecciones

Paso 1: Dictado. You will hear a series of sentences. Listen carefully and write the missing words. (Check your answers in the Appendix.)

1. C F Yo no _____ edad para votar.

2. C F Yo tenía edad para _____, pero no

   _____.

3. C F Para mí _____ importante que

   _____ mucha gente.

4. C F Yo _____ que _____

   uno de los candidatos que _____,

   ¡pero sí _____!

5. C F No se _____ ningún candidato que

   me _____ o me entusiasmara de

   verdad.

6. C F En mi estado no _____ clases en

   las escuelas primarias para que los salones de clase

   _____ de lugares de votación.

BORICUA[a]
¡INSCRIBETE[b] Y VOTA!
QUE NADA
NOS DETENGA[c]
1-800-596-VOTA

[a]Puertorriqueño/a [b]Register
[c]Que... *Let nothing stop us*

Paso 2. Now pause and circle **C** or **F** for each statement in **Paso 1**. No answers will be given. The answers you choose should be correct for you!

Now resume listening.

B. Encuesta: Hablando de la escuela secundaria. You will hear a series of statements about what your life was like in high school. For each statement, circle **C** or **F**. No answers will be given. The answers you choose should be correct for you!

1. C F   3. C F   5. C F   7. C F   9. C F

2. C F   4. C F   6. C F   8. C F

C. ¿Qué esperaba? Answer the following questions using the oral cues.

1. ¿Qué esperaba Ud. que hiciera el robot antes de la fiesta?

   MODELO: (*you hear*) lavar las ventanas → (*you say*) Esperaba que lavara las ventanas.

   a. ... b. ... c. ... d. ...

2. ¿Qué esperaba Ud. que hicieran los invitados durante la fiesta?

   MODELO: (*you hear*) bailar → (*you say*) Esperaba que bailaran.

   a. ... b. ... c. ... d. ...

D. Recuerdos de un viaje. Imagine that you have recently returned from a trip abroad, and your friends want to know all the details. Tell them about some of the things you had to do, using the oral cues. Begin each sentence with **Fue necesario que...** ¡OJO! You will be using the past subjunctive in your answers.

1. ... 2. ... 3. ... 4. ...

E. ¿Qué quería Ud.? Imagine that you are never happy with your family's plans. What would you rather have done? Use the oral cues to tell what you preferred. Begin each sentence with **Yo quería que...**

> MODELO: (*you see and hear*) Ayer cenamos en un restaurante. (*You hear*) en casa →
> (*you say*) Yo quería que cenáramos en casa.

1. Ayer vimos una película.
2. El mes pasado fuimos a la playa.
3. Anoche miramos un programa de televisión.
4. Para mi cumpleaños, me regalaron un estéreo.
5. Esta noche mi madre sirvió patatas en la cena.

49. More About Expressing Possession (Part 2) • Stressed Possessives

A. Gramática en acción: ¿El futuro del mundo? You will hear a series of questions about the following cartoon. Circle the letter of the best answer for each, based on the cartoon. First pause and read the cartoon caption.

Algún día, hijo mío, todo esto va a ser tuyo.

1. a. los seres (*beings*) humanos   b. los seres mecanizados

2. a. a su hijo   b. a nadie

3. a. al mundo en el que vive el robot   b. al mundo del pasado

Now resume listening.

B. Lo mío y lo tuyo

Paso 1. You will hear a brief conversation between Beto and Anita who are arguing about their bikes. Then you will hear a series of statements. Circle **C**, **F**, or **ND**.

1. C F ND

2. C F ND

3. C F ND

4. C F ND

Paso 2. Your friend will make a series of statements about things that she has or about members of her family. Each will be said twice. React to each statement using the written cues. You will need to conjugate the verbs.

> MODELO: (*you hear*) Mi auto es nuevo y económico.
> (*you see*) ser viejo y gasta mucha gasolina →
> (*you say*) Pues el mío es viejo y gasta mucha gasolina.

1. tener poca memoria   3. ser arquitecta   5. estar escritas a máquina (*typed*)
2. vivir en el campo   4. no funcionar

C. En el departamento de artículos perdidos y encontrados. You will hear a series of questions. Each will be said twice. Answer in the negative.

   MODELO: (you hear) ¿Es de Ud. esta maleta? → (you say) No, no es mía.

   1. ...   2. ...   3. ...   4. ...   5. ...

UN POCO DE TODO | (Para entregar)

A. En el periódico. You will hear a series of headlines from a Hispanic newspaper. Each will be said twice. Listen and write the number of each headline next to the section of the newspaper to which it belongs. First, listen to the list of sections.

_____ Sociales	_____ Política	_____ Clasificados
_____ Deportes	_____ Negocios	_____ Espectáculos (*Entertainment*)

B. *Listening Passage:* Resumen de las noticias

Antes de escuchar. You will hear a news brief on the radio, just as it would be if you were listening to it in a Hispanic country. After you listen to the passage, you will be asked to complete the following statements about it. Pause and scan them now to get a general idea of the information to look for.

Noticia 1: Fuerte maremoto en _____, de más de _____ puntos en la escala Richter.

Noticia 2: Tema: _____   Mes: _____

Noticia 3: Visita de Juan Carlos I, _____ de _____. Duración de la visita: _____

Noticia 4: Propuesta del partido de oposición para _____ el precio de la

_____, el _____ y el _____, el

primero en un _____ por ciento y los dos últimos en

un _____ por ciento. El próximo noticiero de amplio reportaje será a

las _____.

Now resume listening.

Listening Passage. The following words and phrases appear in the passage.

el mediodía	*noon*	el paro	*unemployment*
la redacción	*editorial desk*	la propuesta	*proposal*
el maremoto	*seaquake*	el apoyo	*support*
sin hogar	*homeless*	nos sintonicen	*you tune in to us (our broadcast)*

Después de escuchar. Now complete the statements in **Antes de escuchar.**

C. Descripción: Escenas actuales. You will hear the following cartoon caption. Then you will hear a series of questions. Each will be said twice. Answer based on the cartoon and your own experience. Pause and write the answers.

—Lo bueno de las campañas políticas
es que no te las pueden repetir.

1. _____

   _____

2. _____

   _____

3. _____

   _____

4. _____

   _____

D. Y para terminar... Entrevista. You will hear a series of questions. Each will be said twice. Answer based on your own experience. Pause and write the answers.

1. _____

2. _____

3. _____

4. _____

5. _____

6. _____

Paso 1. La tertulia. In the following conversation, Manolo, Maricarmen, and Paco get together for a **tertulia,** an informal discussion of various topics. Today they are discussing politics. Read the conversation along with the speakers.

MANOLO: Muy bien, ¿de qué hablamos hoy?

MARICARMEN: Hablamos del partido político de Paco. Y este, como siempre, cree que los líderes políticos de su partido tienen el derecho de dictar cómo viven los demás. Y yo, claro, no estoy de acuerdo.

PACO: Maricarmen, te equivocas. Es todo lo contrario. Mira. Mi partido ofrece soluciones razonables a los problemas más graves de hoy.

MANOLO: Hasta cierto punto, estoy de acuerdo con Maricarmen. ¿Viste las noticias del Canal 2 anoche? Paco, tu querido partido quería votar cuanto antes la nueva legislación, para que nadie más pudiera protestar.

PACO: ¡No, señor! No es así. ¿Siempre crees todo lo que dicen la prensa y la televisión? ¡Ojalá el asunto fuera tan sencillo!

MARICARMEN: Pero Paco, no me parecen razonables las soluciones propuestas por tu partido. Es verdad que necesitamos nuevas leyes laborales, pero estas no resuelven nada.

PACO: ¡Al contrario! Maricarmen, el anterior presidente no había hecho nada en los últimos años. Mira las noticias. Hay huelgas, desempleo, desastres económicos...

MANOLO: ¡Paco! ¿Tú siempre crees todo lo que dicen la prensa y la televisión?

PACO: Pues, ¡parece que lo único en que estamos de acuerdo es en que *no* estamos de acuerdo!

Paso 2. Aplicación. Now you will participate in a similar conversation, partially printed in your manual, in which you will express your own opinions. Use the following phrases to begin your statements. Pause and write the answers. Answer based on your own opinions. No answers will be given. First, listen to the phrases.

Bueno, pero yo (no) creo que...   Lo siento, pero yo pienso que...

Eso suena (*sounds*) bien, pero...   Sí, pero...

Estoy de acuerdo...

PERSONA 1: Creo que el actual presidente no ha hecho nada para mejorar las condiciones económicas del país.

UD.: _____ 1

PERSONA 2: ¿Y qué tal su política exterior (*foreign policy*)? Creo que es un desastre.

UD.: _____ 2

PERSONA 3: Pues yo pienso que es el mejor presidente que hemos tenido en varios años. El problema es el Congreso. Siempre se opone a las reformas que propone el presidente.

UD.: _____ 3

---

*This **Minidramas** video clip is available on the DVD to accompany *Puntos de partida*, Eighth Edition.

PRUEBA CORTA

A. Apuntes. You will hear a brief paragraph that tells about a political campaign. Listen carefully and, while listening, write the information requested. Write all numbers as numerals. First, listen to the requested information. (Check your answers in the Appendix.)

el nombre de la candidata que perdió las elecciones: _____

el nombre del candidato que ganó las elecciones: _____

el porcentaje (*percentage*) de ciudadanos que votó por la candidata que perdió: _____

la cuestión (*issue*) principal de la campaña: _____

B. Cosas de todos los días: Comentarios sobre la política y los acontecimientos. Practice talking about politics, using the written cues. When you hear the corresponding number, form sentences using the words provided in the order given, making any necessary changes or additions. Use the indicative or the subjunctive, as appropriate. ¡OJO! You will need to make changes to adjectives and add articles and prepositions, if appropriate.

MODELO: (*you see*) 1. ciudadanos / insistían en / que / gobierno / gobernar /
responsablemente (*you hear*) uno →
(*you say*) *Los* ciudadanos insistían en que *el* gobierno *gobernara* responsablemente.

2. queríamos / que / reporteros / informarnos / acontecimientos
3. candidatos / esperaban / que / público / apoyarlos
4. todos / insistían en / que / gobierno / castigar / criminales
5. dudaban / que / gobierno / poder / economizar
6. nadie / quería / que / haber / huelga
7. a / políticos / les sorprendió / que / huelga / durar / tanto / meses
8. era increíble / que / empleados / pedir / aumento / tan / grande

CAPÍTULO **18**

VOCABULARIO | Preparación

A. Encuesta: ¿Qué hizo Ud. en su último viaje? You will hear a series of questions about what you did on your last trip. For each question, check the appropriate answer. No answers will be given. The answers you choose should be correct for you!

1. ☐ Sí ☐ No   6. ☐ Sí ☐ No

2. ☐ Sí ☐ No   7. ☐ Sí ☐ No

3. ☐ Sí ☐ No   8. ☐ Sí ☐ No

4. ☐ Sí ☐ No   9. ☐ Sí ☐ No

5. ☐ Sí ☐ No   10. ☐ Sí ☐ No

B. Definiciones. You will hear a series of definitions. Each will be said twice. Write the number of the definition next to the word or phrase that is best defined by each. First, listen to the list of words and phrases.

_____ viajar a otro país   _____ el huésped

_____ el formulario de inmigración   _____ la frontera

_____ la nacionalidad   _____ el pasaporte

C. Descripción. Identify the following items when you hear the corresponding number. Begin each sentence with **Es un...** , **Es una...** , or **Son...**

1. ...   2. ...   3. ...   4. ...   5. ...   6. ...   7. ...   8. ...

D. Descripción. Describe what these people are doing, using the written cues and the verbs you will hear for each segment of the drawing. Use present progressive forms (**estar** + **-ndo**).

1. los pasajeros   2. los turistas   3. el turista   4. el inspector   5. el turista

■■■Los hispanos hablan: Una aventura en el extranjero

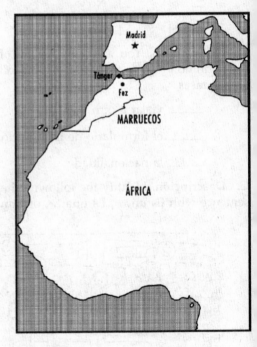

You will hear Clara's story of a trip to the city of Fez, which is in Morocco (**Marruecos**). The story is divided into two parts. The first time you listen to the story, try to get the gist of the narration. Then listen again, or as many times as necessary, for specific information. After you hear each part of the story, pause and answer the true/false items.

Parte 1. The following words and phrases appear in the first part of the story.

hacer transbordo	*to change planes*
Tánger	*Tangiers*
la plaza	el asiento
el croquis	*sketch*

1. C F Clara viajó a Marruecos para estudiar árabe.

2. C F Clara tomó un vuelo directo de Madrid a Fez.

3. C F El vuelo de Madrid a Tánger fue fácil.

4. C F El aeropuerto de Tánger era muy moderno.

Now resume listening.

Parte 2. The following words and phrases appear in the second part of the story.

el destino	*destination*	chapurreado	*poor*
se levantasen	*they got up*	el sello	*official stamp*
las hélices	*propellers*	a punto de estallar	*about to explode*

1. C F Clara usó el color de su tarjeta de embarque para saber qué vuelo tomar.

2. C F Todo—el avión, el aeropuerto, el pasajero que se sentó con ella—tenía aspecto de película.

3. C F Cuando llegó a Fez, Clara ya había pasado por la aduana.

4. C F El padre de Clara ya estaba en el aeropuerto de Fez cuando el avión de su hija aterrizó (*landed*).

Now resume listening.

PRONUNCIACIÓN Y ORTOGRAFÍA **Nationalities**

A. Repeticiones. Repeat the following names of countries and the nationalities of those who were born there.

1. Nicaragua, nicaragüense
el Canadá, canadiense
los Estados Unidos, estadounidense
Costa Rica, costarricense
2. la Argentina, argentino
el Perú, peruana
Colombia, colombiano
Bolivia, boliviana
3. el Uruguay, uruguayo
el Paraguay, paraguaya
4. Honduras, hondureño
Panamá, panameña
el Brasil, brasileño
5. Guatemala, guatemalteca
Portugal, portugués
Inglaterra, inglesa

B. Los países y las nacionalidades. Now you will hear a series of nationalities. Each will be said twice. Repeat each and write the number of the nationality next to the country of origin. First, listen to the list of countries.

_____ Chile   _____ el Ecuador

_____ El Salvador   _____ Venezuela

_____ Puerto Rico   _____ Israel

C. Repaso general: Refranes

Paso 1. Pause and match the number of the Hispanic proverb with its English equivalent. ¡OJO! There is no equivalent English proverb in some cases, just a literal translation.

a. _____ He who sleeps gets swept away.

b. _____ There is an exception to every rule.

c. _____ Every cloud has a silver lining.

d. _____ Everything has a purpose.

e. _____ Nothing is impossible.

f. _____ The early bird catches the worm.

g. _____ Tell it like it is.

1. Llamar al pan, pan y al vino, vino.
2. El agua para bañarse, el vino para beberse.
3. Quien mucho duerme, poco aprende.
4. No hay mal que por bien no venga.
5. No hay regla sin excepción.
6. No hay montaña tan alta que un asno cargado de oro no la suba.
7. Camarón que se duerme, se lo lleva la corriente.

Now resume listening.

Paso 2. When you hear the corresponding number, read the proverbs. Then listen to the correct pronunciation and repeat it.

1. Llamar al pan, pan y al vino, vino.
2. El agua para bañarse, el vino para beberse.
3. Quien mucho duerme, poco aprende.
4. No hay mal que por bien no venga.
5. No hay regla sin excepción.
6. No hay montaña tan alta que un asno cargado de oro no la suba.
7. Camarón que se duerme, se lo lleva la corriente.

D. Dictado. You will hear a series of sentences. Each will be said twice. Write what you hear. Pay close attention to punctuation. (Check your answers in the Appendix.)

1. _____

2. _____

3. _____

    _____

4. _____

    _____

5. _____

GRAMÁTICA

50. Expressing What You Would Do • Conditional Verb Forms

A. Gramática en acción: El viaje de sueños de Yolanda Torres-Luján. You will hear Yolanda, a very busy businesswoman, describe what she would do with some time off. Then you will hear a series of statements. Circle the number of the statement that best summarizes her description.

1.   2.   3.

B. ¿Qué harían para mejorar las condiciones? Using the oral and written cues, tell what the following people would like to do to improve the world.

    MODELO: (*you hear*) Gema   (*you see*) eliminar las guerras →
                 (*you say*) Gema eliminaría las guerras.

1. desarrollar otros tipos de energía
2. construir viviendas para todos
3. resolver los problemas domésticos
4. eliminar el hambre y las desigualdades sociales
5. protestar por el uso de las armas atómicas

C. ¿Qué haría Ud. en Madrid? When you hear the corresponding number, tell what you would do in Madrid. Use the written cues.

    MODELO: (*you hear*) uno   (*you see*) quedarse en un buen hotel →
                 (*you say*) Me quedaría en un buen hotel.

2. comunicarse en español
3. ir al Museo del Prado
4. conocer la ciudad
5. comer paella

D. ¡Entendiste mal! Make statements about your plans, using the written cues when you hear the corresponding numbers. Make any necessary changes or additions. When your friend Alicia misunderstands your statements, correct her. Follow the model.

    MODELO: (*you see*) llegar / trece / junio →
                 (*you say*) UD.: Llegaré el trece de junio.
                 (*you hear*) ALICIA: ¿No dijiste que llegarías el tres?
                 (*you say*) UD.: No, te dije que llegaría el trece. Entendiste mal.

1. estar / bar / doce
2. estudiar / Juan
3. ir / vacaciones / junio
4. verte / casa

51. Hypothetical Situations: *What if . . . ?* • *Si* Clause Sentences

A. Gramática en acción: ¿Qué desean estas personas?

Paso 1. You will hear a series of statements that the following people made regarding what they would like to do if certain conditions were true. Write the number of the statement below the appropriate drawing. ¡OJO! There is an extra statement.

a. _____   b. _____   c. _____

Paso 2. ¿Qué haría Ud.? Now pause and complete the following sentences according to your own preferences. You will be using the conditional tense. No answers will be given.

1. Si tuviera dinero, _____

2. Si pudiera, _____

3. Si me dieran un aumento de sueldo, _____

4. Si viviera en México, _____

5. Si tuviera más tiempo, _____

Now resume listening.

B. Situaciones. You will hear three brief situations. Circle the letter of the best reaction to each.

1. a. ...regresaría a casa en autobús.   b. ...llamaría a la policía.
2. a. ...escribiría un cheque.   b. ...me ofrecería a lavar los platos.
3. a. ...trataría de negociar con el líder del sindicato (*union*) laboral.   b. ...despediría (*I would fire*) a todos los empleados.

C. Descripción: ¿Qué haría Ud.? You will hear a series of statements. Each will be said twice. Write the number of each statement next to the appropriate drawing. First, pause and look at the drawings.

a. _____

b. _____

c. _____

d. _____

e. _____

f. _____

D. Consejos. Imagine that your friend Pablo has a problem with his roommates. What would you do in his place? Answer, using the oral cues.

     MODELO: (*you hear*) llamar a mis padres → (*you say*) Si yo fuera Pablo, llamaría a mis padres.

1. ...   2. ...   3. ...   4. ...

A. De vacaciones en el extranjero. You will hear a brief paragraph describing a series of actions and events. Number the actions listed below from one to ten in the order in which they occur in the paragraph.

First, listen to the list of actions.

_____ aterrizar (*to land*) en Madrid

_____ hacer las maletas

_____ recoger los boletos

_____ despegar (*to take off*) otra vez

___9___ pasar por la aduana

___1___ visitar la agencia de viajes

_____ ir al hotel

_____ sentarse en el asiento del pasillo (*aisle seat*)

_____ bajar del avión

___5___ hacer escala en Londres (*London*)

Now resume listening.

B. *Listening Passage:* **La vida de los exiliados**

Antes de escuchar. Pause and do the following prelistening exercise.

Entre las personas de diferentes nacionalidades hispánicas que viven en los Estados Unidos, los cubanos forman un grupo importante. Conteste las siguientes preguntas sobre la comunidad cubanoamericana.

1. ¿Dónde viven los cubanoamericanos, principalmente?

   _____

2. Muchos cubanos llegaron a los Estados Unidos dentro de un corto período de tiempo. ¿Por qué emigraron?

   _____

3. ¿Qué tipo de gobierno existe en Cuba hoy día? ¿Cómo se llama la persona que gobierna Cuba actualmente?

   _____

4. ¿Pueden los ciudadanos norteamericanos viajar libremente a Cuba?

   _____

Now resume listening.

Listening Passage. Now you will hear a passage about the immigration of a Cuban family to the United States. The following words appear in the passage.

por si fuera poco	*as if that were not bad enough*
el internado	*internship, residency*
el comercio	*business*
echamos de menos	*we miss, long for*
que en paz descanse	*may she rest in peace*

Después de escuchar. Circle the letter of the phrase that best completes each statement, based on the listening passage.

1. Esta familia, como muchas otras familias cubanas, llegó a los Estados Unidos...
   a. a principio de los años ochenta.
   b. hace poco.
   c. a principio de los años sesenta.
2. Emigraron porque...
   a. no estaban de acuerdo con el gobierno.
   b. no tenían trabajo.
   c. tenían problemas con la discriminación.
3. Al llegar a Florida...
   a. todo fue fácil para ellos.
   b. el esposo pudo encontrar trabajo como médico.
   c. fue necesario que el esposo tuviera dos trabajos.
4. Los padres todavía...
   a. echan de menos su país.
   b. quisieran vivir en la Cuba de Fidel Castro.
   c. piensan que fue un error salir de Cuba.

Now resume listening.

C. En el periódico: Viajes. The following ad appeared in a Mexican newspaper. You will hear a series of statements about the ad. Circle **C** or **F**. First, pause and scan the ad.

RIVIERA:
PAQUETES
¡OFERTA ESPECIAL!

VACACIONES...?
Venga con su familia al Hotel Riviera del Sol de Ixtapa y disfrute de un merecido descanso en las soleadas playas y tibias aguas del espléndido Pacífico Mexicano y ahorre con nuestros tradicionales:

¡¡¡PAQUETES RIVIERA...!!!

"RIVIERA, PAQUETE DE PRIMAVERA"
3 NOCHES
4 DIAS
CON TRES DESAYUNOS
Precio por persona:
$ 80,000.00
Noche Extra:
$ 28,000.00

"PAQUETE MINI RIVIERA DE PRIMAVERA"
2 NOCHES
3 DIAS
CON DOS DESAYUNOS
Precio por persona:
$ 58,000.00
Noche Extra:
$ 28,000.00

1. C F   2. C F   3. C F   4. C F

D. Y para terminar… Entrevista. You will hear a series of questions. Each will be said twice. Answer based on your own experience. Pause and write the answers.

1. _____
2. _____
3. _____
4. _____
5. _____
6. _____

VIDEOTECA   Minidramas*

Paso 1. En la agencia de viajes. In this conversation, Lupe and Diego visit a travel agency. Read the conversation along with the speakers.

AGENTE: ¿Ya tienen alojamiento en Mérida?

LUPE: No, todavía no. Buscamos un hotel que sea decente, pero que tampoco sea muy caro. No tenemos el dinero para pagar un hotel de lujo.

AGENTE: Entiendo. Muy pocos estudiantes tienen mucho dinero. Bueno, les puedo ofrecer habitaciones en varios hoteles a precios muy razonables. A ver… ¿Cuándo piensan hacer el viaje?

DIEGO: La última semana de mayo.

AGENTE: Ajá… Eso va a estar un poco difícil. Casi todos los hoteles estarán completamente ocupados durante esa semana. Si viajaran una semana más tarde, encontrarían más habitaciones desocupadas.

LUPE: Bueno, está bien. Entonces, la primera semana de junio.

AGENTE: Excelente. Les puedo ofrecer dos habitaciones individuales con baño privado en el hotel Estrella del Mar. No es un hotel de lujo, pero es bueno y muy lindo. El precio por cada habitación es de 150 pesos por noche.

LUPE: Perfecto.

AGENTE: Y, ¿cuántos días piensan quedarse?

DIEGO: Unos cuatros o cinco días, nada más. Yo soy de California, y debo regresar pronto.

AGENTE: Muy bien. Tienen habitaciones reservadas para la primera semana de junio. ¿Sus nombres, por favor?

DIEGO: Sí, cómo no. Yo me llamo Diego González y la señorita es Guadalupe Carrasco.

AGENTE: Muy bien.

DIEGO: Gracias.

Paso 2. Aplicación. Now you will hear a similar conversation, partially printed in your manual, in which you play the role of the **viajero.** Complete the conversation using the written cues. Pause and write the answers. Write out all numbers. First, listen to the cues for your conversation. ¡OJO! The cues are not in order.

muchas gracias

556

la pensión María Cristina

uno o dos meses

aquí lo tiene

---

*This **Minidramas** video clip is available on the DVD to accompany *Puntos de partida*, Eighth Edition.

AGENTE: Pasaporte, por favor.

VIAJERO: _____.¹

AGENTE: ¿En qué vuelo llegó?

VIAJERO: En el _____²

AGENTE: Y, ¿cuánto tiempo piensa permanecer (*to remain*) en el país?

VIAJERO: Pienso quedarme _____³

AGENTE: ¿Tiene una dirección aquí en la que se le pueda localizar?

VIAJERO: Sí, cómo no. Estaré en _____,⁴ la Calle del Prado, número 27.

AGENTE: Está bien. Puede pasar.

VIAJERO: _____.⁵

PRUEBA CORTA

A. **¿Qué haría Ud. si... ?** You will hear a series of questions. Answer, using cues chosen from the following list. First listen to the list. ¡OJO! There is an extra cue.

> confirmar las reservaciones
> declarar mis compras
> conseguir un pasaporte
> ir a la pastelería
> alojarme en un hotel de lujo
> ir a la oficina de correos

1. ...   2. ...   3. ...   4. ...   5. ...

B. **Las finanzas.** You will hear the following sentences. Restate each, using the conditional.

MODELO: (*you see and hear*) No le ofrecerán el puesto a menos que tenga buenas
recomendaciones. →
(*you say*) Le ofrecerían el puesto si tuviera buenas recomendaciones.

1. No le harán el préstamo a menos que esté trabajando.
2. No ahorraré más dinero a menos que controle mis gastos.
3. No pagaré las cuentas antes de que reciba el cheque semanal.
4. No te cobrarán el cheque hasta que lo firmes.

C. Y para terminar... Entrevista final. You will hear a series of questions, or situations followed by questions. Each will be said twice. Answer based on your own experience. Model answers will be given for the last two questions. Pause and write the answers.

1. _____

2. _____

3. _____

4. _____

5. _____

_____

_____

_____

_____

_____

_____

6. _____

_____

_____

_____

_____